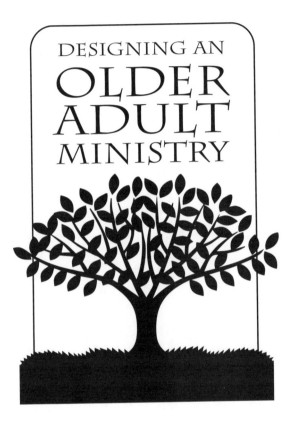

DESIGNING AN
# OLDER ADULT
## MINISTRY

Richard H. Gentzler, Jr.

**DISCIPLESHIP** RESOURCES

P.O. BOX 340003 • NASHVILLE, TN 37203-0003
www.discipleshipresources.org

*††††*

Reprinted 2000.

Cover and book design by Sharon Anderson

ISBN 0-88177-269-0

Library of Congress Catalog Card No. 98-88814

DR269

# TABLE OF CONTENTS

113264

※

## CHAPTER FIVE: SUGGESTED RESOURCES

## CHAPTER SIX:
## SAMPLE FORMS AND OTHER HELPS

## CHAPTER ONE
# INTRODUCTION

## WHY A MINISTRY BY, WITH, AND FOR OLDER ADULTS?

Until rather recently in human history, few people grew old. Most people did not reach old age; they died! In many cases, middle-aged people were not even concerned about aging parents. Their parents had long since died.

The life expectancy in ancient Rome and Greece was about twenty years. In medieval Europe, the average life expectancy was thirty years. In 1900, the average life expectancy in the United States had risen to forty-seven years. By 1990, the average life expectancy in the United States was seventy-five years.

We are an aging society! More people are living longer and better today than ever before. In 1900 there were three million people age sixty-five and older. This figure accounted for four percent of the total population. By 1990, this same older population numbered 31.6 million. This represented 12.5 percent of the total United States population, or about one in every eight Americans. (See chart on aging trends in the United States, page 10). In the year 2000, there will be 34.7 million people age sixty-five and older. Within thirty years, by the year 2030, this number of older people will double to 69.4 million.

More people are living longer today than ever before. As a result of modern medical technology, better nutrition, reduced job risks, and hosts of other variables, the life expectancy for people in the United States is increasing. We are quickly moving away from a youth-oriented culture to an "elderculture," where older adults will outnumber the children and youth in our society. What this means, and the impact this will have, can only be guessed. In order to help our society make this adjustment, we need to rethink what it means to be an older adult.

Aging is a natural process in living. From the moment of conception and birth, we begin to age. There is nothing unnatural, demeaning, or morbid about growing older. It is not a disease. It is a part of life, a part of God's wonderful creation. God's good gift of life includes aging.

Everyone ages differently, however. There are no two older adults who are exactly alike. Through the years, people with different genetic backgrounds and different life experiences age in many and various ways. As a result, older adults are perhaps the least homogeneous group of any age cohort. Each has had different social, educational, physical and biological, emotional, and religious experiences over the years.

How we age is affected by several factors. These include the lifestyle we have lived, the amount of exercise we have received, the way we have handled stress, the foods we have eaten, and many other factors. Heredity is another important factor, particularly in defining characteristics of our physical appearance—such as balding or graying hair.

But not only is our society aging; so is our church. A study by the General Council on Ministries in the mid-1990's concluded that approximately sixty-two percent of the membership in The United Methodist Church was fifty years of age or older. In all probability, this percentage will continue to rise as society continues to experience a myriad of changes, not least of which are the changing age demographics.

The myths of aging would have us conclude that all older adults are economically disadvantaged and physically frail. We often believe that older people are ready to disengage from society and are content to sit at home alone while waiting for death to release them from the confines of their misery! In the past, this view provided most churches with the following two options for ministry: (1) ignore older adults while engaging in "real" ministry with other age groups; (2) provide only a ministry *to* and *for* older adults. Meaningful ministry *with* older adults was not envisioned because of ageism and ignorance on the part of church leaders. The church viewed its older-adult ministry through a narrow interpretation of ministry. It emphasized a ministry *to* and *for* older adults to the exclusion of any other form of older-adult ministries.

Yet, as we look at older adults around us, we see that the majority are healthy, active, and involved in life. We are often guilty of stereotyping older adults. Contrary to popular opinion, most older adults are in relatively good health. Although many older adults suffer from chronic illness, as many as seventy-one percent indicate that their health is good to excellent.

Another common myth is that all older adults move into nursing homes, where they wait for their impending death. Contrary to this popular yet misguided belief, not all older people are living in nursing homes. While approximately five percent of the elderly population live in institutions, ninety-five percent do not!

Many older adults today are continually involved in the world around them. They are an active, energetic, and growing people. They seek out new opportunities for learning and involvement in peace and justice issues. They want to make a difference in the life of their family, community, and world. The church that breaks free from the paralyzing grip of ageism will find an exciting and challenging ministry before it. Churches that are intentional about older-adult ministry know that ministry today is a ministry *by* and *with*, as well as *to* and *for*, older adults.

✺

With the growing number of older adults in our society, it is becoming increasingly more evident that older people are, and will continue to be, diverse and heterogeneous in their wants and needs. Gerontologists (those who study and work with aging populations) note that people do not suddenly change their interests and behaviors as they grow older. People responsible for teaching or developing programs and seminars for older adults must do a careful analysis of the needs and wants of this group, just as they would with any other group. Perhaps an examination of some common patterns of growing older would be helpful in making such an analysis.

Older adults, no less than other people, have special needs and strengths. As one ages, one must give more attention to maintaining health and compensating for declining physical vigor. For many people, as a result of the loss of family and friends through death and moves, loneliness is confronted with a harshness never before imagined. Indeed the world of the older adult undergoes major shifts. New roles must be adopted and former roles adapted.

Over the years older adults experience many types of losses. They experience physical loss, which may bring about limitations relative to the level of impairment. They may experience sensory changes: vision, hearing, taste, touch, and smell. There may be a loss of energy, muscle tone, and mobility.

Most older adults will face the prospects of retirement and must adjust to the social and financial changes that retirement introduces. Sometimes housing becomes an issue and new living arrangements must be considered. Many older adults also experience a loss of independence, self-worth, and meaning in their life. Needless to say, it would be inappropriate for us to ignore the impact that losses make upon the life of older adults. It is impossible for us to adequately serve the needs of older adults without understanding these losses.

While losses are very much a part of their life, many older adults desire to come to terms with their losses. They want to make sense out of their life and find purpose in living. Psychologist Erik Erikson stated that this is a normal and healthy stage of life that he described as Ego Integrity versus Despair. Older adults invest time in life review and reminiscence to integrate past experience with present situation. They look at "the good, the bad, and the ugly" in their life and conclude, "This has been my life; this is who I am."

In addition, older adults desire to share not only their memories but also their wisdom and experience with others. Erikson described this stage as Generativity versus Stagnation. Older adults want to give back to society and give some of themselves to others, often beyond their family. Older adults want to be appreciated for their uniqueness and accepted in spite of their physical limitations. Like most everyone else, they want to be needed and loved and often seek out opportunities to be in service to others.

Although the issues that older adults face cannot be minimized, the majority of older adults feel satisfied with life. Obviously there are some real strengths associated with older people. They are survivors! They have experienced the harsh realities of life and have persevered, carried on, and moved forward. In the future, older adults will become even more involved with the activities of life as they continue to break free from the barriers, the myths, and the stereotypes that bind them.

Although the church cannot ignore its great responsibility in helping meet the needs of the frail or at-risk elderly, neither can we ignore the involvement of healthy older adults in ministry. It is imperative that we in local church congregations take seriously our responsibility for an intentional ministry by, with, and for older adults.

This book will help you and your church get started. As you read through this manual, you will find helpful ways to design older-adult ministries in your church. You have an awesome responsibility, but I trust that God will use you and bless your every effort for the good of all God's people!

# AGING POPULATION TRENDS IN THE UNITED STATES

(Compares population of adults sixty-five years and older to population of children and teenagers)

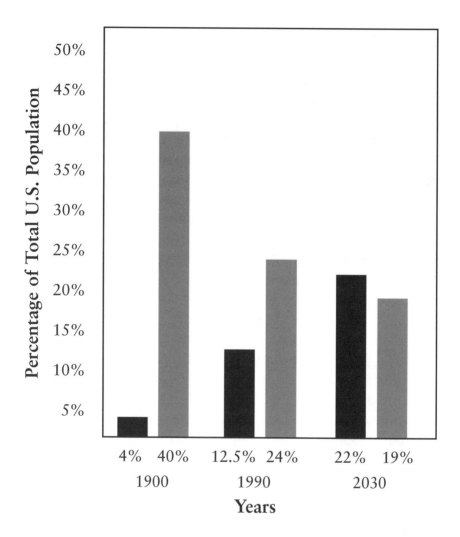

Adults 65 years and older

Children and Teenagers

# ATTITUDES ABOUT AGING

## Societal Attitudes

In some societies, when a person is fifty-nine years old, that person might stretch the truth and claim to be sixty-two years old. In the United States, if a person is sixty-two years old, the person may stretch the truth and claim to be fifty-nine years old. Some societies place greater respect and higher value on the worth of older people. For Americans, aging is often seen as something to be denied, ignored, or avoided. Billions of dollars are spent each year by people who want to maintain a "youthful" image. Cosmetics, surgery, and apparel are just a few of the many ways people in our society spend money to keep looking young.

Society for a long time has held up the image that youthfulness, strength, and beauty are good qualities and that people who are older, weaker, and more wrinkled are less desirable. However, in an increasingly "graying" society, I believe that aging will become valued and respected. With many more older adults, especially with the coming wave of Baby Boomers, our understanding of aging and aging issues will shift dramatically.

Retirement at age sixty-five was said to be set by the German leader Otto Von Bismarck during the Industrial Revolution because hardly anyone lived beyond that age. He felt that if you reached sixty-five, you were entitled to some leisure before you died. In 1935 when Social Security was enacted in the United States, life expectancy was around sixty-two. Congress set the age of sixty-five as the time older workers could begin receiving Social Security. Perhaps Congress believed that few people would live long enough to collect it. Today, people can still receive full Social Security benefits when they reach sixty-five, yet life expectancy is no longer sixty-two but rather seventy-six! What does this mean to a society that has a large number of older adults collecting Social Security and fewer younger and middle-age workers who pay into it?

Perhaps many employers will abandon the age-sixty-five retirement model, hiring workers to do jobs as long as they can.

In addition, in the near future many more people will live past age one hundred. Given that, there's no reason to regard sixty-five as a normal retirement age. The idea that people should do nothing for one-third of their life, even if they have enough money to do so, becomes ridiculous.

Church leaders need to be aware of public policy issues (that is, Social Security, Medicare, Medicaid, and so forth) that have an impact on the life of older adults in our society.

## Personal Attitudes

Because we live in an "age-denying" society, our personal attitudes about aging are often shaped by societal attitudes. As children we are delighted to tell others our age, and even advance it a little bit. For example, instead of just saying, "I'm four," a child might say, "I'm four and a half." As we grow older, it isn't uncommon to hear people say, "It's no one's business to know how old I am." As a result, particularly if children and youth are present, growing older is often portrayed as something to be ashamed of or feared. Below are several personal views of aging that exist in our society.

**Resistance**—when people deny their own aging. When asked how old they are, they might respond, "It's none of your business." They may spend hundreds or thousands of dollars each year to not look their age. They resist aging by denying that they are growing older.

**Resignation**—when people give in to aging. Instead of seeking helpful adult dependencies, these people give up. Their motto is, "I'm eighty years old; I should be feeling or acting this way." They often say, "I'm too old to try something new." They believe that life has lost its meaning, and they are now ready to die.

**Relaxation**—when people sit in "rocking chairs" and stay put. Some people look forward to retirement so that they can finally sit all day in the rocking chair. They believe that they deserve to be able to just rest. They live with the false assumptions that leisure is more fulfilling than Christian service and that God no longer uses older adults.

**Recreation**—when people want to play golf every day. God didn't create us to spend our later years walking a golf course or watching television fourteen hours a day. Many people look forward to retirement so that they can play. Unfortunately, after playing eighteen holes of golf five days a week, many older adults begin to feel that their life is empty. They no longer find playing golf or watching television all that fulfilling.

**Relocation**—when people move. Sometimes older adults relocate to a warmer climate. Sometimes they move to be closer to family, friends, or amenities. And sometimes they move because they must, whether as a result of physical, economic, or social conditions.

**Reinvention**—when people create new work opportunities. Many older adults never knew they had certain talents and abilities until after they retired. They were so busy doing what they had to do that they never had time to explore latent talents or to try something new. As they grow older, some people discover that they enjoy painting, woodcarving, gardening, writing, and so forth. Perhaps an increasingly important criterion for the choice of avocations and hobbies of older adults will be their potential for generating future income.

**Renewal**—when people grow in faith in God through Jesus Christ. Many older adults were so busy working or raising families that they never had time to deepen their spiritual life. Even though they may have worshiped regularly and participated in the life of the faith community, growing in faith has become a lifelong endeavor throughout the many changes in their life. One is never too old to be in need of God's grace and wisdom. Those wise enough to pursue this need will offset their days not only through self-actualization but also through spiritual fulfillment.

## Church Attitudes

At one time the accepted practice within The United Methodist Church was to give older-adult church members an honorary status on boards and committees. The church wrongfully believed that only younger adults had new ideas and sharper minds for the work of the church. While older adults are no longer given honorary status on boards and committees, unfortunately ageism is still quite prevalent in The United Methodist Church.

Let me pose this question to you: If you have an older couple or widow attend your worship service on a given Sunday morning and on that same Sunday morning you have a young family visiting, do you give as much energy and resources to reach the older couple or widow as you do the young family? Many churches, when they are honest, will say they give more energy trying to reach the young family than they do trying to reach the older couple or widow. Why? If we all stand in need of God's grace, isn't it important for all God's children to be brought into the faith community? Does God value one over another? Of course not, and neither should the church!

Often in churches that are experiencing a change in pastoral appointment, ageism and age discrimination are prevalent. Many staff/pastor-parish relations committees in conversation with the district superintendent will seek a pastor who is thirty-five years old and has thirty years of experience! They believe that only a younger person is able to lead their church or is capable of providing a vision for the future. If people are living longer and healthier today, why is the church still operating under erroneous assumptions about aging? Why is retirement age for clergy set at seventy? Likewise, why is ordination withheld from people after the age of seventy? At eighty years of age, Moses was called to lead God's people out of bondage and slavery in Egypt. I wonder where God's people would be today if the Hebrew children had said to God, "No thank you, God; we'll wait for a younger man or woman to come along and lead us."

The church is one institution in our society that can and should take the lead in dispelling the false notions and paralyzing myths about aging. The church has a responsibility to say to society and individuals that all people are valued and have worth in the eyes of the church.

## Biblical Attitudes

Aging, like learning, is a continuous process in life. In the Creation story, God blesses all that God has made (Genesis 1:31). When a person reaches the age of sixty-five, our faith teaches us that God does not take away God's blessing. In fact, the Scriptures are quite clear in stating that God uses older adults for God's purpose and mission. Abraham is seventy-five years old when he is commanded by God to leave his home (Genesis 12:1-4). And, as noted before, Moses is eighty years old when he speaks to Pharaoh after God appears to him in the form of a burning bush (Exodus 3:1-12 and 7:1-7).

In 1 Samuel 3, Eli provides us with a glimpse of intergenerational learning. The boy Samuel has never heard the voice of God. One night God visits Samuel; but Samuel, in his youthfulness, fails to recognize that it is God calling him. Eli, who is old, teaches Samuel that the voice he hears is God. Likewise, Paul (the elder) teaches Timothy (the young man) the importance of spiritual growth and of conveying God's word to others (1 Timothy 4).

The Bible suggests that long life is a gift from God. It is a reward for faithfulness. As the writer of Proverbs says,

> Gray hair is a crown of glory;
>   it is gained in a righteous life. (Proverbs 16:31)

Isaiah also makes it clear that God will watch over and protect those who are old:

> Listen to me, O house of Jacob, . . .
> even to your old age I am he,
>   even when you turn gray I will carry you.
> I have made, and I will bear;
>   I will carry and will save. (Isaiah 46:3-4)

Sometimes in the Bible there were fears associated with aging:

> Do not cast me off in the time of old age;
> do not forsake me. (Psalm 71:9)

At other times, aging was a blessing. Remember the story of Simeon in the Temple when Jesus was presented by his parents? Simeon praised God saying,

> Master, now you are dismissing your servant in peace,
> according to your word;
> for my eyes have seen your salvation. (Luke 2:29-30a)

On occasions Jesus was confronted with aging issues. Once Nicodemus came to him and said, "How can anyone be born after having grown old? Can one enter a second time into the mother's womb and be born?" (John 3:4). Another time, Jesus reveals the kind of death Peter will experience: "Very truly, I tell you, when you were younger, you used to fasten your own belt and to go wherever you wished. But when you grow old, you will stretch out your hands, and someone else will fasten a belt around you and take you where you do not wish to go" (John 21:18).

Although the Judeo-Christian tradition rejects what some religious cultures call ancestor worship, the Bible does place great importance on children honoring their parents (Exodus 20:12; Proverbs 1:8, 20:20, 23:22; Ephesians 6:2). Should children fail in their obligation to their parents, there are no words more condemning than,

> The eye that mocks a father
> and scorns to obey a mother
> will be pecked out by the ravens of the valley
> and eaten by the vultures. (Proverbs 30:17)

And in the Apocrypha we read:

> My child, help your father in his old age,
> and do not grieve him as long as he lives;

even if his mind fails, be patient with him;
because you have all your faculties do not despise him.
(Sirach 3:12-13, Apocrypha)

Finally, the Bible suggests that wisdom and beauty are associated with older adults:

Wisdom is with the aged;
understanding in length of days.
(Job 12:12, RSV)

The glory of youths is their strength,
but the beauty of the aged is their gray hair.
(Proverbs 20:29)

For old age is not honored for length of time,
or measured by number of years;
but understanding is gray hair for anyone,
and blameless life is ripe old age.
(Wisdom of Solomon 4:8-9, Apocrypha)

# THE CHURCH'S POSITION

Both in 1992 and 1996, General Conference of The United Methodist Church approved legislation mandating the formation of the United Methodist Committee on Older Adult Ministries (see ¶1119 in *The Book of Discipline of the United Methodist Church—1996*.) The committee, with representatives from various general boards and agencies, jurisdictions, the Council of Bishops, and the central conferences, is administratively related to the General Board of Discipleship. This committee, with its connectional relationships, has great and far-reaching implications for the work of older-adult ministries in each local church congregation, district, and annual conference.

Prior to the passage of this important legislation, the 1988 General Conference approved a resolution encouraging the church to become aware of aging issues and to develop older-adult ministries. In addition to providing information about aging, the resolution outlined specific tasks for local churches and annual conferences. The resolution reads in part:

1. Each local church is called upon to:

(a) Become aware of the needs and interests of older people in the congregation and in the community and to express Christian love through person-to-person understanding and caring;

(b) Affirm the cultural and historical contributions and gifts of ethnic minority elderly;

(c) Acknowledge that ministry to older persons is needed in both small and large churches;

(d) Ensure a barrier-free environment in which the elderly can function in spite of impairments;

(e) Motivate, equip, and train lay volunteers with a dedication for this important ministry;

(f) Develop an intentional ministry with older adults that:

i. ensures each person health service, mobility, personal security, and other personal services;

ii. offers opportunities for life enrichment including intellectual stimulation, social involvement, spiritual cultivation, and artistic pursuits;

iii. encourages life reconstruction when necessary, including motivation and guidance in making new friends, serving new roles in the community, and enriching marriage; and

iv. affirms life transcendence, including celebration of the meaning and purpose of life through worship, Bible study, personal reflection, and small-group life;

(g) Recognize that older persons represent a creative resource bank available to the church and to involve them in service to the community as persons of insight and wisdom (this could include not only ministry to one another, but also to the larger mission of the Church for redemption of the world, including reaching the unchurched);

(h) Foster intergenerational experiences in the congregation and community including educating all age groups about how to grow old with dignity and satisfaction;

(i) Ensure that the frail are not separated from the life of the congregation but retain access to the sacraments and are given assistance as needed by the caring community;

(j) Provide guidance for adults coping with aging parents;

(k) Cooperate with other churches and community agencies for more comprehensive and effective ministries with older persons, including radio and television ministries;

(l) Accept responsibility for an advocacy role in behalf of the elderly; and

(m) Develop an older-adult ministry responsible to the council on ministries involving an adult coordinator or older-adult coordinator, volunteer or employed. (An older-adult council may be organized to facilitate the ministry with older adults.)

2. Each annual conference is called upon to:

(a) Provide leadership and support through its council on ministries for an intentional ministry to older persons in its local churches, with special attention to the needs of women and minorities;

(b) Develop a program of job counseling and retirement planning for clergy and lay employees;

(c) Share creative models of ministry and a data bank of resources with the local churches and other agencies;

(d) Define the relationship between the annual conference and United Methodist-related residential and nonresidential facilities for the elderly, so that the relationships can be clearly understood and mutually supportive;

(e) Relate to secular retirement communities within its boundaries;

(f) Recruit persons for professional and volunteer leadership in working with the elderly;

(g) Serve as both a partner and critic to local church and public programs with the elderly, promoting ecumenical linkages where possible;

(h) Support financially, if needed, retired clergy and lay church workers and their spouses who reside in United Methodist long-term care settings;

(i) Promote Golden Cross Sunday and other special offerings for ministries by, for, and with the elderly; and

(j) Recognize that other persons within the conference, both lay and clergy, represent a significant and experienced resource that should be utilized in both the organization and mission of the conference.

(From *The Book of Resolutions of The United Methodist Church—1996*. Copyright © 1996 by The United Methodist Publishing House; pages 172–174. Used by permission.)

# CHAPTER TWO
# FACTS AND FEELINGS ABOUT AGING

## GETTING IN TOUCH WITH AGING:
## EXPLORING MYTHS AND REALITIES

The church, one institution in our society with a high percentage of older-adult members, has a great opportunity to think and minister creatively. It is important, then, as we develop an intentional ministry by, with, and for older adults, to come to terms with our own aging: both the parts we look forward to and the parts we fear.

Before going on, stop and complete "Facts About Aging: A Quiz," on pages 65–66. When you have completed the quiz, check your answers using pages 67–68. To help you reflect on your personal views concerning aging and older adults, complete the "Self-Awareness Inventory," on page 22.

# SELF-AWARENESS INVENTORY

Using the key below, circle the letters on the word scale that best express your feelings.

> **Key:** A = I strongly agree with the word on the left.
> B = I agree with the word on the left.
> C = I am neutral about either word.
> D = I agree with the word on the right.
> E = I strongly agree with the word on the right.

Ask the question, "When I think of older people, I think of people who are . . ."

| | | |
|---|---|---|
| Kind | A B C D E | Uncaring |
| People-centered | A B C D E | Self-centered |
| Friendly | A B C D E | Grumpy |
| Lonely | A B C D E | Sociable |
| Wealthy | A B C D E | Poor |
| Weak | A B C D E | Strong |
| Greedy | A B C D E | Generous |
| Rigid | A B C D E | Tolerant |
| Active | A B C D E | Inactive |
| Bitter | A B C D E | Hopeful |
| Wise | A B C D E | Foolish |
| Ill | A B C D E | Healthy |
| Happy | A B C D E | Sad |
| Unchangeable | A B C D E | Changeable |
| Forward-looking | A B C D E | Backward-looking |
| Fast | A B C D E | Slow |
| Close-minded | A B C D E | Open-minded |

# PERSONAL REFLECTION

After you have completed the Self-Awareness Inventory, think about older adults you know. Who are they? Are they family members, friends, neighbors, or colleagues? Do you see them in your responses to your Self-Awareness Inventory? How do you feel about older adults? How do you feel about your own aging? Does your attitude about aging come from society, from personal experience, from the church, from the Bible, or from any combination of these? Take time to reflect on these questions. If possible, review your Self-Awareness Inventory with others. How are your views similar to theirs? How do your views differ from theirs?

As you consider your responses to both the Self-Awareness Inventory and the above questions, you become aware that there are few, if any, right answers. Older adults are uniquely created and wonderfully individualistic. Some older adults are kind, some are uncaring, and many fall somewhere in the middle. Some are people-centered, some self-centered, and some Christ-centered. The purpose of the Self-Awareness Inventory is to invite you, the reader, into an honest appraisal of your own feelings about aging. By sharing your views with others, you open yourself up to new learning and growth.

Now, consider what you have learned about aging from these sources. Select a person whom you consider an example of successful aging.

- What do you admire most about this person?
- What do you learn from this person about the negative experiences of growing older?
- What do you learn from this person about the positive experiences of growing older?

Reflect again on ways this person models successful aging. How do you see yourself aging now? in five years? in ten years? beyond ten years?

# KINDS OF OLDER ADULTS

Who are the older adults who are part of our congregations and who live in our communities?

**1. Healthy/Active.** These are the older adults who are active and involved in the life of our faith community. They may be members of the choir, participants in the Bible study class, neighbors in the pew, leaders in the church. They are the ones the church depends upon for volunteer service and ministry.

**2. Ill/Active.** These are the ones who want to continue participating in the life of the church but because of changing health conditions find it difficult. They try to stay involved whenever possible and may become increasingly discouraged when they are not able to participate in a church-sponsored activity.

**3. Transitionally Impaired.** These may be the healthy/inactives who for a variety of reasons feel forced to adopt new roles or adapt to changes. They may have recently experienced the death of a spouse or significant other. Physical changes following a stroke or incontinence may impede an otherwise active lifestyle. The faith community plays an important role in helping these people become healthy/active again. If not, they may become part of the next group, the homebound.

**4. Homebound.** These people are unable to regularly participate in activities outside their home. This group of older adults were once referred to as shut-ins. Because of the negative connotations of the word *shut-in* (often meaning shut out from life), many sensitive congregations use the word *homebound* to refer to people who are increasingly confined to their homes.

**5. Residents of Healthcare Facilities.** These people may be healthy/active, ill/active, transitionally impaired, homebound and frail, in need of skilled medical and/or psychiatric nursing care, and/or dying. Residents of healthcare facilities and retirement communities represent a broad range of older adults.

**6. Institutionalized.** These are older people who are confined in our jails and prisons. Prison populations are growing with increasing numbers of older people.

**7. Dying.** These older adults may be in their homes, in hospitals, in nursing homes, and so forth. As a result of their acute illnesses, they may have the support of hospice care or some other form of caregiving assistance.

## LOSSES ASSOCIATED WITH AGING

Over the years, older adults experience many types of losses. It is helpful to be aware of these losses:

**1. the loss of significant loved ones** (the death of a spouse, parents, a child or children, siblings, close friends, pets);

**2. the loss of aspects of self** (self-esteem, vision, hearing, taste, smell, hair, teeth, muscle tone, energy, and so forth);

**3. the loss of external objects** (job, home, income, automobile and/or driver's license, and so forth);

**4. the loss of time** (so much to do, yet little time remaining to do it; fewer years left to accomplish dreams and goals);

**5. the loss of independence** (dependent on gadgets, aids, other people);

**6. the loss of purpose** ("What do I do now with my life?"; questioning one's worth; loss of a dream).

While losses are very much a part of their life, many older adults desire to come to terms with their losses. They want to make sense out of their life and find purpose in living. In a very real way, older people often struggle to find a deeper acceptance of themselves. They may have a strong desire to share not only their memories but also their wisdom and experience with others. Like all people, they want to be needed and loved and often seek out opportunities to be in service to others.

# GAINS ASSOCIATED WITH AGING

Aging is a process involving the whole life span from conception and birth to death. It is something we all experience. For some of us, the process is longer than for others.

*Gerontophobia* is a word meaning the fear of aging. Unfortunately, pastors, no less than lay people, may have difficulty accepting their own aging. When we see no potential gain or good in aging, we may fear what is before us. Pastors experiencing difficulty with their own aging may treat older adults with indifference or avoidance or as children. It is important, therefore, that the church begin to rethink its theology of aging and explore again the wealth of material in the Bible that speaks encouragingly and hopefully of growing older.

Gerontologists (people who study patterns and effects of aging) have generally believed that "successful" aging is the result of one of two theories:

- **Disengagement Theory:** Successful aging involves the gradual withdrawal of aging people from social networks, and a concurrent tendency for others to lower their expectations of aging people and to reduce interaction with them.
- **Activity Theory:** Successful aging results from the positive outcomes of aging people remaining engaged in the world at large, and others finding substitute roles for those that are lost through retirement, widowhood, and so forth.

## Another Theory: The Continuity Theory

Today many leaders of older-adult ministries believe that there is a need for selective engagement and disengagement and that the proper amount of activity depends upon the individual. The important point is that older adults, no less than other people, should have the right to choose the direction and the scope of their involvement in a meaningful life.

Older adults must help the church overcome its fear of aging. Ageism (discrimination based solely on one's age) is clearly evident in our church and society today. The church needs models of successful aging for its young and old alike—

models of successful aging that come from the ranks of both clergy and laity; models that demonstrate to both the church and the world that aging is a gift from God and that older people can be as creative, inventive, and "alive" as younger people. While older adults need to model successful aging, the church must be a faith community that accepts older adults and encourages them in their interdependency with others.

Potential gains in aging include

**1. discovering helpful adult dependencies** (eyeglasses, hearing aids, walkers, wheelchairs, medication, and so forth);

**2. relaxing one's defenses** (no longer climbing the corporate ladder, no longer needing to compete for position or status);

**3. redefining one's status** (no longer known for your occupational status, married status, and so forth);

**4. finding time for spiritual growth** (daily devotions, regular Bible reading, prayers, meditation, fasting, Christian conversation, worship, study);

**5. creating new work opportunities** (enjoying doing things you want to do, not what you have to do);

**6. serving/helping others** (tutoring children, volunteering in an elementary school, visiting homebound people, providing transportation, preparing meals, offering respite care, and so forth);

**7. sharing one's faith and life journey** (living out one's faith, teaching others about the Bible, recording on video or audiocassette one's faith journey, journaling, writing prayers and litany for worship and devotion, and so forth);

**8. growing in wisdom.** (People do not become wise simply because they are old. However, as you will see on the next page, older people have the greater potential to become wise.)

# WISDOM OF THE AGING

Wisdom often abounds in older adults. But wisdom is not something people receive just because they have reached a certain age. Nor is wisdom attained simply by reading volumes of books or by participating in continuing education classes. Wisdom can be possessed by the educated and uneducated alike.

Wisdom is not a capacity to solve all human problems or even to understand them fully. And not everyone who is an older adult is necessarily gifted with wisdom. But over time, through the many and various experiences of life, older adults can have an ability to view problems, to appreciate them, and to see them in their wholeness.

In former agrarian societies, a person could be considered wise or as having wisdom simply by living through the seasons. With the many changes in our world today—especially in the areas of technology, telecommunications, and information—younger people often seem to have more knowledge. Where does this leave older adults? How are older adults in our society viewed as having wisdom today? I believe that the answer lies not so much in technological or scientific knowledge as in spiritual knowledge. Older adults have the potential to grow in mature faith, to deepen their relationship with God through Jesus Christ. This experience is wisdom. The church would do well to tap this maturity of faith and find ways older adults can model and share their faith with others.

## MAJOR FACTORS IN THE WELL-BEING OF OLDER ADULTS

In designing an intentional ministry by, with, and for older adults, it is important to know the major factors that contribute to the well-being of older people. Ideally, ministry with older adults will provide key elements that will enhance and promote each area of well-being. Ask the question, What can our local congregation do to improve and support older adults in the areas of

1. **health:** the mental and physical conditions of older people;

2. **economic resources:** the financial resources needed by older people to maintain their independence or to care for the needs of others;

3. **social and leisure activities:** involving older adults in fitness and recreational programs;

4. **socio-economic achievements:** the educational and occupational status of older adults;

5. **interpersonal relationships:** the availability of supportive family and friends;

6. **spirituality:** the level of commitment to and importance of faith and religion in one's life.

## FAITH NEEDS OF OLDER ADULTS

Just like other people, older adults have faith needs. Unless these needs are met, older adults will be hampered from gaining a deeper relationship with God through Jesus Christ. Older adults need to

1. **know that God loves older people.** While the church sings "Jesus Loves the Little Children" (and Jesus does!), the church must remember that Jesus loves older people, too. God loves and blesses people throughout the whole life span. No one is ever too old to stand in need of God's grace.

2. **experience a church that cares about older adults.** While this may sound easy enough, sometimes this knowledge is lost or never fully realized when local congregations emphasize children, youth, or family ministries to the exclusion of other forms of ministry. Older adults need to experience respect and acceptance and to feel valued by the church.

3. **remain a vital part of the church.** Older adults can continue to make valuable contributions to the church's ministry. The highest percentage of financial giving in many churches comes

from older people, who give nearly twenty percent more than others in the church. In addition, forty-two percent of people age sixty or older attend religious services weekly compared to only twenty-five percent of adults under age forty. Churches depend upon the generous gifts of older people, but many older people want to make significant contributions to the ministry of the church beyond financial giving. Still other older people, many of whom are on fixed incomes, are not able to make financial contributions to the church as they once did. Although making financial contributions is important, the church needs to provide other ways for older adults to remain vital to the life and ministry of the church.

**4. find new ways of serving others.** Serving as mentors and role models for the benefit of succeeding generations is important, and older adults can do this even when their health and physical strength decline. But it is also important for the church to provide new opportunities that help frail older adults feel empowered for ministry.

**5. have available support systems.** Coping with losses, adopting new roles, and adapting to changes can be difficult for people of any age. It is very important that older adults have available support systems that help them cope with the many changes in their life.

# CHAPTER THREE
# FORMING A WORKING COUNCIL

## DESIGNING AN OLDER-ADULT MINISTRY

As we face the prospect of an aging society, and therefore an aging church, we must begin to find new ways for ministry. Perhaps the best way to begin is by capitalizing on the splendid resource we already have, namely older adults. We begin with our strength. Older adults have experienced the realities of life and have persevered. As a valuable resource, they hold the keys to the future of our church. Unfortunately, many church leaders ignore the important role of older-adult ministry. They see older adults as rigid, conservative, and unchanging. These same leaders are ready to announce that the church is "dying," even though many congregations are filled with older adults. They fail to realize that there are exciting opportunities for ministry by, with, and for older adults.

As we dispel the many myths and stereotypes associated

with aging, we become aware of the great possibilities for ministry among older adults. Beyond simply knowing the positive aspects of aging, we must begin providing opportunities for older-adult ministry. In this chapter, we will address the process local congregations can take to develop intentional ministry by, with, and for older adults. The following ten steps are helpful in designing a methodology for ministry.

**Step 1: Organize an older-adult council.**

If you have an interest in older-adult ministries, begin by finding another person who shares your hopes and dreams. As the two of you discuss your ideas for ministry, think of others who might also share your vision. Invite these people to your meeting. You may also want to contact your pastor or other professional staff for suggested names of interested people.

When you have between six and fifteen people (depending upon the age demographics and membership size of your local church), organize an older-adult council (or committee, depending upon your church policy). In order to have a diversity of older adults, the council should be composed of a cross section of older women and men (married, single, divorced, widowed, homebound, various races and ethnicities, and so forth). One or two younger adults who are concerned about aging issues and older-adult ministry may also serve on the council. It is important to go through proper church channels to establish the legitimacy and authority of the council as well as to secure financial support. If possible, get a line item for older-adult ministries in your church budget.

**Step 2: Gather information about older adults.**

As a council, develop a survey instrument for gathering information about the older adults in your local church. In designing a survey form, include questions to help you obtain the following information: (1) name, address, telephone number, and other general information; (2) needs and concerns of older adults; (3) ways older adults can use their talents in ministry with others. It is important to know as much about the older adults in your congregation as possible. Be thorough in asking the right kinds of questions. (See the sample "Older-Adult Survey Form," on pages 69–72.)

After you have developed the survey form, you will want to interview all the older adults in your congregation. Begin by compiling a list of all the older adults on the church roll and members of church organizations not on the church roll. Remember, because of ageism and age discrimination in our society, some older adults will be offended that you are identifying them as older adults. You need not apologize for your efforts; rather, help people understand the positive attributes of being an older adult. Until we better educate people of all ages about gerontological issues, there will be people who live in anger and denial about their own aging.

After compiling a list of all the older adults in your congregation, invite your pastor to send a letter to them. Your pastor should inform the older adults about the older-adult survey being done in the church. In addition, place announcements in the weekly bulletin and/or the church newsletter explaining the reason for the interviews, the dates interviews will be conducted, the survey instrument, and the interview process. Train council members to visit older adults. Invite older adults to receive into their homes a trained council member who will share the survey form with them. If additional people are needed for interviewing older adults, train other church members to help with the task. Invite older youth, young adults, and other adults to help with the interview process. Remember to call each older adult ahead of time to set a day and time for their visit.

Interviewers should have a general knowledge of the process of aging. Use this manual as a guide to help train them. Select interviewers who are warm and friendly, people generally interested in the well-being of others. Interviewers must be honest, have a high level of integrity, be supportive of the ministries of the church, and be able to maintain confidentiality.

At the time of the interview, give a copy of the survey form to each person being interviewed. By receiving a copy of the survey instrument, older adults will feel more comfortable about the interview process. Remember to smile, exhibit a friendly attitude, and keep personal information confidential. Take no longer than is needed to complete the survey form, about thirty minutes. Do not take stewardship materials, church offering envelopes, or the church budget with you. This is not an appropriate time to push church financial matters onto older adults. They may suspect that you have an ulterior motive or hidden agenda about the visit. Depending upon need and areas of concern, you may want to survey all the older adults in your town, village, or neighborhood.

The least effective way to obtain the desired information is to send your survey form through the mail. Often these survey forms are not returned. People receiving the forms may not know what to do, or the form may be lost or misplaced. You are likely to have only ten to twenty percent of the forms returned, far from a clear picture about the needs and talents of the older adults in your faith community. In order to design an intentional ministry by, with, and for older adults, every older adult should be visited where he or she resides.

During your visit, explain to the older adults that the church is concerned with supporting them in their Christian discipleship; responding to their needs; enabling them to use their talents and experiences in helping others; and developing an effective ministry by, with, and for older adults.

## Step 3: Review existing church programs.

Review church programs and activities from the past year. Identify all those that involved older adults. The purpose of this step is to become familiar with the programs in your church that already involve older adults. Evaluate the effectiveness of these programs and determine whether the activities are ongoing events. As a council, examine whether or not any of the activities should be discontinued or changed. (See "Local Church Program Assessment Form," on pages 73–76.)

You may also want to more clearly identify a particular program your congregation already provides for older-adult ministry. The purpose of such a survey is to identify the purpose, leadership, and cost of such a program, as well as to help evaluate its effectiveness. (See "Local Church Program Event Survey Form," on pages 77–78.)

**Step 4: Survey community social service agencies.**

Encourage council members to visit the social service agencies in your community, such as the area Agency on Aging. Take a survey of their programs and services. Discover what is already going on in the local community. If a community social service agency is providing a program that is meeting the needs of older adults, don't try to compete. Find ways your older adults might help with ongoing programs. In addition, identify areas of unmet needs, those that community social service agencies are unable to implement, and see whether you have the available resources to meet these needs. (See the "Community Social Service Agency Survey Form," on pages 79–80.)

**Step 5: Develop a program of ministry for your church.**

After you have interviewed the older adults in your church (and in the community when this is an appropriate goal), evaluated existing church programs, and identified community social service agency programs, you are now ready to design a program of ministry for your local church. As a result of your thorough study and investigation, you may discover several programs that need to be developed and implemented. At this point the council will need to list, prioritize, and select which program or programs it will implement first.

**Step 6: Establish a shared vision and set goals and objectives.**

You may have several good ideas for ministry. Establish a shared vision: a vision that everyone on the council is able to state clearly. This may take the form of a mission statement. It may also include a specific ministry model. It is important that everyone is clear about the vision of older-adult ministry in your congregation. In addition, goals will identify who will be involved, what programs will be initiated, where programs are to take place, and when programs are to happen. Objectives will identify how you plan to accomplish your goals. The council will want to give much thought to this step. Having a shared vision that is in agreement with your goals and objectives will help you realize a successful program.

**Step 7: Identify resources and key people.**

What resources are needed to get the job done? Where can we turn for assistance in getting the necessary resources? Who can best help us implement our program? Who is capable of providing leadership for our event? The council will need to discuss the best possible resources and key people for the program. Leave no stone unturned. Be thorough and resourceful. As you review your program needs, seek out the best resources and most qualified people.

**Step 8: Involve other churches and agencies when appropriate.**

Sometimes our resources are not great enough or we are better able to get the work done by involving other churches or agencies. Identify and invite other churches and agencies to become involved. Combine forces for getting the program started. Do not compete for the same audience; rather, work together. If you are a small-membership church, involve other churches on your charge or in your area. If your community is large enough, you may wish to involve the larger community.

**Step 9: Implement your program.**

Begin by establishing a timeline for implementing the program. Identify the various steps along the way. List the resources to be used. Develop a checklist to make sure goals and objectives for the program are being met.

**Step 10: Evaluate.**

Periodically, the council should evaluate its goals and objectives to determine the effectiveness of your vision for the program. If the program is warranted, continue the program. If the program is not working, begin the process over again.

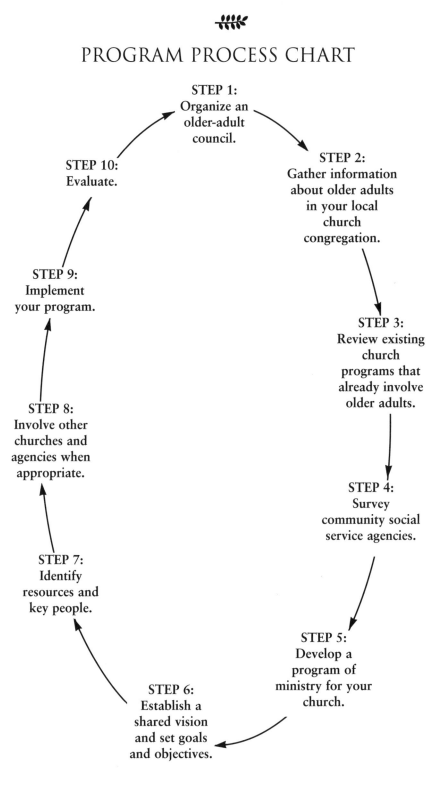

# PROGRAM PROCESS CHART

STEP 1:
Organize an
older-adult
council.

STEP 2:
Gather information
about older adults
in your local
church
congregation.

STEP 10:
Evaluate.

STEP 3:
Review existing
church
programs that
already involve
older adults.

STEP 9:
Implement
your program.

STEP 8:
Involve other
churches and
agencies when
appropriate.

STEP 4:
Survey
community social
service agencies.

STEP 7:
Identify
resources and
key people.

STEP 5:
Develop a
program of
ministry for your
church.

STEP 6:
Establish a
shared vision
and set goals
and objectives.

✿✿✿✿

# A MODEL MINISTRY:
# OLDER-ADULT COUNCIL

Designing an intentional older-adult ministry is an essential ingredient in helping laity live out the mission of the church. The United Methodist Church understands its mission as "making disciples of Jesus Christ." (*The Book of Discipline of The United Methodist Church—1996*. Copyright © 1996 by The United Methodist Publishing House; page 115. Used by permission.) In order to fulfill the mission, each church has the responsibility for

- reaching out into its community and receiving all people into the faith family;
- encouraging people in their relationship with God and inviting them to commitment in Jesus Christ;
- providing opportunities for people to be nurtured and to practice the disciplines of the Christian faith;
- supporting people to live and act as faithful disciples in the world, empowered by the Holy Spirit.

As we think about the mission or primary task of the local church congregation, several questions come to mind:

- How can a local church reach out to older adults in its community?
- How can the church help older adults experience a new or renewed relationship with God through Jesus Christ?
- What are the best ways to help nurture older adults in the Christian faith?
- How can the local church best support older adults as they live and act as faithful disciples in the community?

The following steps will help a local church congregation plan its ministry with older people.

**1. Get started.**

If you are the coordinator for older-adult ministries (or an equivalent position) in your local church, you will want to be familiar with your role. (See "Job Description: Local Church Coordinator of Older-Adult Ministries," on pages 81–83.)

## 2. Organize an older-adult council.

As indicated earlier, the older-adult council should be composed of six to fifteen members, depending upon the size of the congregation. The majority of the members should be older adults. Each member is invited to serve for one year. The local church coordinator for older-adult ministries may serve as chairperson or may instruct the council to choose a chairperson from within the group. If the council chooses to elect a chairperson from the group, the coordinator for older-adult ministries will serve on the council as a resource person.

Include representation on the council from the many different types of older adults in your congregation: women, men, various races and ethnicities, those who are single, those who are widowed, those who are divorced, and so forth. It is also a good idea to have one or two adults under sixty-five years of age on the council. Please note: Although younger adults may be on the council, refrain from using them in key leadership positions. The leadership for such a group should be the direct responsibility of older adults.

The council should have a chairperson, a vice chairperson, and a recording secretary, each with a one-year term of office. In addition, committees and special task forces may be organized to better complement the goals and objectives of the council.

The small-membership church may find that there are simply not enough people to establish an older-adult council. Do not dismiss the possibility of an older-adult council simply because you believe that your church membership is not large enough to warrant its existence. Through investigation you may learn that there are opportunities for older adults to serve in your community. It may be helpful for you to expand your concept of an older-adult council and include people from the community.

An older-adult council can be developed with leadership from several churches (a multiple charge, a circuit, a cluster of churches in the same geographical area, and so forth). Sometimes we are able to minister more effectively together than we are by ourselves!

## 3. Define the responsibilities of the council.

As the council on older-adult ministries begins to meet, there will be many questions, such as, What do we do now? In order to provide direction for your ministry, read the list of responsibilities below. After you have spent some time together and have identified a shared vision, you will want to prepare a mission statement. This statement should be in line with the mission statement of your local church. For example, if the mission statement for First United Methodist Church is "to make disciples for Jesus Christ," then the mission statement for the council on older-adult ministries might be "to provide opportunities for undergirding the faith development of older adults for the transformation of the world." Spend time as a council developing your mission statement. Remember to keep your mission statement short in length (perhaps no more than one or two sentences) so that it is memorable and can be easily recalled.

The role of the local church council on older-adult ministries is to

- **study** the needs of older adults in the congregation;
- **interview** all the older members of the congregation. This may be done by using a survey form. Consider having members of the council visit the older adults of the congregation (and where possible, all the older adults in your community).
- **discover** what older adults in the congregation need, think, feel, believe, and so forth. Find out what is on their minds. What do they think of the church, its ministries, their community, and themselves?
- **develop** programs that meet the needs of the various older-adult members of the church and community;
- **identify** needed resources and key people for implementing programs;
- **meet** on a regular basis for assessing needs, providing information from reports, planning programs, and evaluating existing and ongoing projects;
- **inform** the pastor and local church governing body as to the planning and program needs of the council;

- **evaluate** existing programs on the basis of effectiveness in older-adult ministries;
- **represent** older adults' concerns to the council on ministries or church council and serve in a liaison capacity as needed with other people and groups within and beyond the local church;
- **attend** various district, conference, and jurisdictional workshops and seminars related to older-adult ministries;
- **advocate** the need for policies, programs, resources, and funding to help meet the needs of older adults;
- **know** the issues and concerns related to older adults, individually and as a group.

**4. Look beyond the local congregation.**

Most church leaders believe that ministry only begins to be ministry when it goes beyond the four walls of the local church. If this is true, then the local church, through the work of the older-adult council, will become involved in community ministry.

There are probably many older adults in your community, as well as people of every age, who could greatly benefit from the services of your church. Your ministry might involve these people through teaching ministries, worship, adult daycare, caregivers service, support groups, meals, transportation, and a host of other activities. (These will be presented in greater detail in "Selected Ministry Program Models," beginning on page 49). It is important to remember to involve older adults in this vital ministry, as participants or recipients or both.

The following suggestions will help you begin to reach out to older adults and their needs in your community.

- **Identify** existing programs by making a community resource list. Check with community and state agencies to see if a list already exists. If not, begin compiling such a list.
- **Contact** other churches and agencies with whom you can combine your efforts. Avoid duplicating what is already being done. Some things can be done better by combining forces.
- **Enlist** the support of key people in the church and community who are involved in older-adult ministries. These people may be resources for information, program leadership, and training.

- **Develop** goals with a timeline for accomplishment. Goals will help you realize the desired ministry you wish to attain. A goal will identify the *who*, *what*, *where*, *when*, *why*, and *how* of your program development.
- **Evaluate** your programs. Set checkpoints for an evaluation of each program. Invite leaders, participants, and planners to evaluate the program.

## LOCAL CHURCH MINISTRY WITH OLDER ADULTS

Periodically every church should review its ministry with older people. If we are not intentional in our efforts, we may find older adults being discouraged from participating fully in the life of the church. For a tongue-in-cheek look at ways we discourage older adults from participating in our faith communities, see "How to Discourage Older Adults From Being Part of Your Congregation," on page 87.

The following questions are intended to help local congregations evaluate their older-adult ministry programs.

### 1. Is the church intentional?

The number of older adults in our society and our congregations is growing. These people, usually identified as either retired or sixty-five years of age or older, have special needs, concerns, and potential. On a regular basis, each congregation should make a needs assessment and resource inventory of its older-adult members. By doing this, a local church can be sure it is providing an intentional ministry by, with, and for older adults.

### 2. Does the church empower older adults for life and ministry?

Older people are active in the life of the church. Their leadership is solicited, welcomed, and used. They are encouraged to take charge of their life and are given primary responsibility for developing and implementing an older-adult ministry.

✸✸✸✸

### 3. Is the church free of barriers for all participants?

All efforts are made to remove physical, psychological, social, and economic barriers so that older adults are better able to participate fully in the life and activities of the church. (For help in determining the physical barriers in your church, see the "Local Church Accessibility Survey Form," on pages 84–86.)

### 4. Does the church reach out to older adults?

In order for ministry to purposefully reach out to all older people, the church includes evangelism, worship, Bible study, outreach, pastoral care, small groups, and Christian education as program offerings for older adults. Support groups, lay shepherding, home and institutional visits, and regular mailings are just some of the efforts being made to keep in regular communication with older people.

### 5. Are concerns of the aging included in the liturgy?

The joys, celebrations, fears, losses, and dreams of older adults are included as an integral part of litanies, prayers, hymns, and sermons. Milestones passed and goals achieved are celebrated. Older adults are encouraged to share their faith and to take an active role in the worship services. Rites of passage (such as retirement) and rituals (such as a house blessing) are provided for the support and ministry of older adults. (For special litanies useful for worship services, see "A Litany on Aging," pages 90–91, and "A Statement of Faith on Aging," pages 92–93.)

### 6. Does the church provide opportunities for continuous growth?

Bible study groups and prayer groups are just some of the opportunities for spiritual guidance. Opportunities for various types of classes, seminars, workshops, and support groups are provided to help with life transitions and to enhance learning.

### 7. Are there opportunities for companionship and socialization?

Older adults have the opportunity to enrich their life through fellowship with others. Through planned activities and events they receive affection, respect, recognition, stimulation, and feelings of self-worth.

## 8. Are many of the church's programs intergenerational?

Older adults have the opportunity to share their faith, experience, and knowledge with people of all ages. Likewise, they have the opportunity to learn from people of other ages. Older people and young people work together on various projects and exchange services for one another.

Intergenerational programming with children or youth and older adults should encourage learning and understanding for each age and stage of life. Listed below are some important elements to keep in mind when planning intergenerational programs:

- Aging is a natural progression in life.
- Aging is not morbid, unnatural, or a disease.
- Each age and stage of life is full of unique potential.
- The older-adult population is a diverse group.
- Stereotypical thinking about older adults may be inaccurate (as may be stereotypical thinking about children and youth).
- God loves and blesses people of all ages.
- People of all ages are called by God into Christian discipleship.
- Children, youth, and older adults can learn from one another.

## 9. Is the church community minded and ecumenical?

Older adults are encouraged to become familiar with the programs and services of their local community and public agencies and when possible are engaged in volunteer service. Support is given to join and cooperate with other congregations to do for older people what cannot be done by individual congregations.

## 10. Does the church address concerns related to social policies and issues?

Older adults are informed about pending legislation, social policies, and other issues that may adversely affect their life as well as the life of other people and generations. They form study groups, task forces, and/or committees, acting as advocates in order to help combat social problems.

## CHAPTER FOUR

# PLANNING PROGRAMS

## THE PLANNING PROCESS

After you have gained an understanding of the aging process, organized an older-adult council, completed the "Older-Adult Survey Form," surveyed the programs of your local church, and learned about your community from local social service agencies, you are ready to develop programs to meet the needs.

The following four important steps may help a local church congregation plan for an effective ministry by, with, and for older adults.

### 1. Define the problem.

- Identify the specific needs of older people in your church and community.
- Identify the specific needs of others in your church and community for whom older adults can develop and participate in an effective ministry.

- Establish priorities.
- Identify available resources.
- Establish goals and objectives.

**2. Develop the program.**
- Plan the appropriate program to meet the specific needs of the proposed objectives.
- Determine the costs.
- Obtain the necessary funding.
- List the tasks to be performed.
- Secure the necessary resources.
- Prepare a program outline, including budget costs and a timeline for completion.

**3. Implement the program.**
- Recruit and train volunteers.
- Enlist the support of the church and community.
- Refine the program proposal.
- Establish evaluation procedures.

**4. Evaluate the program.**
- Collect, organize, and interpret the data.
- Evaluate the effectiveness of the program.
- Continue the program, if it is warranted.
- Begin the planning process again.
- Start a new program.

# MINISTRY MODEL I:
# S.E.N.I.O.R.S. MINISTRY

How we age depends on a variety of factors. Physical and spiritual well-being, educational opportunities, and nutrition and healthcare are just a few of the many variables affecting how people age. In addition, gender, lifestyle, race, heredity, and marital status can profoundly affect age matters. But perhaps the single most important factor is attitude. How we live, respond to, and address issues of aging is often a matter of attitude.

Opportunities abound for older adults to be involved with life in their later years. Your local congregation, district, and annual conference can develop intentional ministries that enhance the life of older adults. Review your church ministry with older adults. Are your programs reaching all your older adults? Here are a few suggestions for a S.E.N.I.O.R.S. program.

## S: Spirituality

- Form Bible study groups, prayer groups, Christian education classes, retreats, journaling classes, worship participation, and so forth.

## E: Education

- Invite special speakers.
- Provide learning opportunities and classroom seminars on topics of general interest, such as gardening, healthcare, financial issues, political and ethical issues, public policy, computers, life review, and so forth.

## N: Nutrition and Health

- Start a program called Congregational Health Ministries. Information about starting such a program can be obtained from Health and Welfare Ministries, General Board of Global Ministries—UMC, 475 Riverside Drive, Room 330, New York, NY 10115.
- Provide opportunities for learning (for example, "cooking for one" classes), regular blood pressure checks, medication information, and so forth.

## I: Intergenerational Opportunities

- Invite people of all ages to participate in programs, events, worship, and learning.
- Provide opportunities for mentoring, visiting, tutoring, and listening. Encourage children and youth groups to visit homebound and nursing home residents. Provide ways for older adults to share their faith journey with children, youth, and young adults.

## O: Outreach/Service

- Provide opportunities for teaching, leading, visiting, and serving. Develop programs that include caregiving, transportation, delivered meals, home chore and minor maintenance, and so forth.
- Provide "Checklist for Selecting a Nursing Home" (pages 88–89) for people who are considering becoming residents of a healthcare facility.

## R: Recreation

- Invite older adults to participate in physical fitness and exercise.
- Provide low-impact aerobics classes, camping, fishing, tennis, and golf outings; travel events and field trips; and so forth.

## S: Social Activities

- Plan fellowship meals, arts and crafts, singing and fun activities, quilting and sewing circles, games, painting, and so forth.

# MINISTRY MODEL II: SHEPHERD'S CENTER

Under the leadership of Dr. Elbert C. Cole, the congregation of Central United Methodist Church in Kansas City, Missouri, developed an important ministry model for serving the needs of older adults in their community. This ecumenical ministry model, which involved the whole community, is called the Shepherd's Center. Today it is a model used by many communities seeking to meet the needs of older people. For more information about this model, contact Shepherd's Centers of America, 1 West Armour Boulevard, Suite 201, Kansas City, MO 64111; phone 816-960-2022 or toll-free 1-800-547-7073; fax 816-960-1083; e-mail staff@shepherdcenters.org; Web site www.shepherdcenters.org.

The Shepherd's Center model organizes the needs of older adults into four categories. Programs are then developed within these four areas.

## 1. Life maintenance needs

All people must have their basic human needs met in order

to survive. These needs include adequate shelter, nutritious meals, healthcare, and financial resources.

Some programs to meet these needs include transportation, delivered meals, financial advice and assistance, telephone reassurance, minor home maintenance, chore service, and caregiving services.

### 2. Life enrichment needs

As people acquire coping and life-enriching skills, they are able to maintain their maximum level of independent living.

Some programs to meet these needs include Christian classes and courses and other educational classes and courses, marriage enrichment courses, and field trips.

### 3. Life reorganization needs

As people experience significant changes in their life, opportunities for life reconstruction or reorganization need to be met.

Some programs to meet these needs include grief support groups; widow-to-widow groups; support groups for caregivers, stroke survivors, cancer patients, and so forth; and workshops on Alzheimer's disease, divorce recovery, adults caring for aging parents, and so forth.

### 4. Life celebration needs

As people wrestle with the meaning of life and death, life transcendence or life celebration needs must be met.

Some programs and resources to meet these needs include providing the sacraments for institutionalized and homebound people, Bible study, worship, prayer groups, devotional materials, and so forth.

## SELECTED MINISTRY PROGRAM MODELS

As you design an intentional ministry by, with, and for older adults, keep in mind that every older adult is a unique individual and that every church is different. It is also important to remember that no model will work exactly alike in two different settings.

## Ministry by Older Adults for Other Older People

**1. Caregiving:** More than four million older adults experience difficulty with at least one activity of daily living, such as walking, dressing, getting in and out of bed, getting around indoors, bathing, and preparing meals. This number is projected to grow to over seven million people by the year 2020. This is approximately one out of every four people sixty years of age and older. Of those people who need daily assistance, approximately one out of three do not have anyone to rely on for help. In a caregiving ministry, older adults provide direct care for people who have difficulty with these activities of daily living.

**2. Friendly Visitors:** Older adults visit people who are ill, homebound, institutionalized, and transitionally impaired.

**3. Telephone Reassurance:** Older adults make telephone calls on a regular or daily basis to other older adults who live alone, making sure they are okay.

**4. Companion Service:** Older adults serve as volunteers who escort people to the doctor's office, drugstore, grocery store, and so forth, helping these people every step of the way and serving as more than just transportation.

**5. Respite Care Service:** Older adults stay with a person who needs constant care and/or attention, thus providing the primary caregiver a break from caregiving.

**6. Home Maintenance and Repair:** Older adults skilled in carpentry, plumbing, painting, and minor odd household jobs provide assistance to people who need such help.

**7. Meal Service:** Older adults prepare and/or provide meals for people who are not able to cook. This may be part of a local church program, part of a meal program such as the national Meals-On-Wheels program, or some other format.

**8. Outreach:** Older adults reach out to other older people and invite them to church activities.

**9. Spiritual Direction:** Older adults serve as leaders and teachers of Bible study programs, Sunday school classes, and other church programs.

**10. Field Trips:** Older adults visit places of interest. These trips may be for education and information, recreation, mission study, or work mission.

**11. Exercise and Fitness Programs:** Older adults conduct and participate in a program of physical fitness. This may be an aerobics class or some other form of exercise well designed for the members of the group.

## Ministry by Older Adults for Others in the Church

**1. Tutoring:** Older adults provide tutoring opportunities for children and youth. This may expand into a ministry beyond the local church.

**2. Calling:** Older adults participate in a variety of calling opportunities such as hospital visitation, nursing home visitation, evangelism efforts, membership renewal programs, stewardship campaigns, and so forth.

**3. Foster Grandparents:** Older adults "adopt" a child. They can enjoy going together to the movies, out to dinner, to school functions, and so forth. This is an important ministry for children who have no grandparents in the area.

**4. Living History:** Older adults share their faith story and life journey by recording it on audiocassette or videocassette or on paper. This often provides important information about the history of the local church and/or community.

**5. Intergenerational Study Groups:** Older adults join with children, youth, and younger adults to study issues of faith and other issues together.

**6. Teaching and Leading:** Older adults participate in teaching and sharing their faith in special classes and group activities.

**7. Counseling Other Generations:** Older adults serve as faith counselors in helping people of other generations.

**8. Prayer Ministry:** Older adults participate in intentional prayer circles and serve as prayer partners for others.

**9. Worship Leadership:** Older adults provide for the religious nurture of themselves and others by participating in leadership or worship.

## Ministry by Older Adults for Others in the Community

**1. Daycare Services:** Older adults sponsor and supervise a child or adult daycare center.

**2. Crime Watch:** Older people provide a "neighborhood watch," notifying authorities in the event of a crime.

**3. Helping Hand:** Older adults sponsor a food, clothing, and/or service bank by providing food, clothing, chore service, and light maintenance for others.

**4. Latchkey Kids Program:** Older adults sponsor a program that cares for neighborhood children before and/or after school in the absence of other adult supervision.

**5. House Sharing:** Older adults develop a program that brings college students into their homes to live in order to help students with the increasingly high cost of education. Students can help with chores, minor maintenance, cooking, and so forth, and in return receive a place to live and companionship at little or no cost.

**6. Marriage Enrichment Program:** Older married couples help other couples make a good marriage better. They can reflect on changes in marital communication as a result of retirement, serious illness, and so forth. The Caring Couples Network® is an excellent program for older married couples. For more information about this program, write to Director, Family Ministries; General Board of Discipleship; P.O. Box 340003; Nashville, TN 37203-0003.

**7. Fine Arts Program:** Older adults are involved in creative drama, music, choir, arts, and hobbies.

# ADDITIONAL SUGGESTIONS
# FOR PROGRAMS AND PROJECTS

As you begin developing programs for older adults, the following suggestions will be helpful for you.

**1. Initially and continuously, use older adults in your planning process.** If possible, develop a council for older-adult ministries and listen to the needs and suggestions of older people in your faith community.

**2. Continue to study the needs of older adults.** Familiarize yourself with aging concerns. Be sure you know who you are trying to reach and why.

**3. Remember that older adults are all different.** Provide a variety of activities and programs in an effort to reach as many older adults as possible. Younger older adults may not want to do the same activities as older ones. Women may want to do different activities than men. Be sensitive to these differences.

**4. Find out what activities older adults want to participate in.** Conduct a survey in order to secure this information.

**5. Do some networking.** Look for people or programs already providing services to older adults. Get input from these sources.

**6. Develop programs that meet the needs of a variety of older adults.** Be sure to include both structured and unstructured activities. You do not have to fill every waking moment with a program.

**7. Coordinate planning, and carry out a variety of activities for older-adult participants.** Make sure that all facilities are accessible to people with a variety of physical abilities and that restrooms are located nearby.

**8. If appropriate, obtain from each older-adult participant basic health information,** including diet restrictions, medication, physician's and family members' phone numbers, and any activity constraints.

**9. Meet on a regular basis** for assessing needs, providing information from reports, planning programs, and evaluating existing and ongoing projects.

**10. Keep informed of issues and concerns relating to older adults.**

Older-adult councils often wonder what type of programs and projects to develop and what topics to discuss at meetings. Listed on the next pages are some suggestions. This is not an exhaustive listing. There are hundreds and thousands of possibilities. However, this information will help you get started in the right direction.

**Aging Issues**
Aging in a rural
  environment
Aging in an urban
  environment
Ethnic/minority groups
  and aging
Men and aging
Women and aging
Adults caring for
  aging parents
Grandparents raising
  grandchildren

**Caregiving**
Respite
National Federation of
  Interfaith Volunteer
  Caregivers
Stephen Ministries

**Communication**
Hearing impaired
Visual impaired
In the family
In the marriage
Between the generations

**Cooking**
Cooking for one
Nutrition
Special diets

**Daycare Centers**
Child
Adult

**Death and Bereavement**
Grief support groups
Widow-to-widow programs

**Elder Abuse**
Emotional
Physical
Financial

## Ethical and Legal Issues
Guardianship
Living will
Power of attorney

## Exercise and Physical Fitness
Low-impact exercise classes
Body recall

## Financial Planning
Estate planning
Investment planning

## Foster Grandparents
Adopting grandchildren
Adopting grandparents

## Future Trends in Aging
Baby boomer aging
Retirement issues

## Health Issues
AIDS/HIV
Alcohol and drug abuse
Alzheimer's disease
Arthritis
Cancer
Chronic illness
Depression
Heart disease
Medication overdose
Strokes
Suicide

## Homebound and Chore Service
Daily telephone checks
Delivery of worship tapes
House repairs
Lawn services

## Marriage and Divorce
Divorce recovery seminars
Marriage enrichment retreats
Caring Couples Network®
Sexuality and intimacy

## Medical Issues
Death with dignity
Powers of attorney
Patients' rights
Medicare and Medicaid

## Minor Maintenance Service
Moving furniture
Cleaning
Appliance repair
Changing light bulbs
Plumbing assistance
Appliance repair
Painting

## Accessibility Issues for the Physically Challenged
Curb cuts
Elevators
Handrails
Parking spaces
Ramps
Wheelchair lifts

## Pre-funeral Planning
Burial plans
Cremation
Insurance policies
Lot selection
Obituaries
Organ or body donation
Planning the service
Wills, trusts, bequests

**Shopping and Deliveries**
Groceries
Drugstore
Clothing

**Social Activities**
Older-adult dinner and
   banquet
Trips and outings
Fellowship meals
Arts and crafts
Films and tapes
Visitation
Discussion groups
Recreation

**Spiritual Growth**
DISCIPLE Bible study
Worship
Prayer
Sacraments
Older-adult recognition

**Transportation**
Doctor's visits
Church services and activities
Pharmacy

**Visitation**
Homebound
Institutionalized
Residents of healthcare
   facilities
Stephen Ministries

Use the space below to list other possibilities for programs and projects for your local congregation and community.

# CHAPTER FIVE
# SUGGESTED RESOURCES

## BOOKS AND PRINTED RESOURCES FOR LEADERS OF OLDER-ADULT MINISTRY

*A Profile of Older Americans—1996* (American Association of Retired Persons and the Administration on Aging, Department of Health and Human Services, 1996).

*A Profile of United Methodists Based on the Survey of United Methodist Opinion* (General Council on Ministries, 1995).

*Aging America: Trends and Projections* (U.S. Senate Special Committee on Aging, American Association of Retired Persons, Federal Council on the Aging, and U.S. Administration on Aging, 1991).

*Aging and God: Spiritual Pathways to Mental Health in Midlife and Later Years,* by Harold G. Koenig (The Haworth Press, Inc., 1994).

‌❦

*Aging: God's Challenge to Church & Synagogue*, by Richard H. Gentzler, Jr., and Donald F. Clingan (Discipleship Resources, 1996).

*Aging, Spirituality, and Religion: A Handbook*, edited by Melvin Kimble, Susan H. McFadden, and all (Fortress Press, 1995).

*Aging Without Apology: Living the Senior Years With Integrity and Faith*, by Robert Seymour (Judson Press, 1995).

*Americans 55 & Older: A Changing Market*, edited by Sharon Yntema (New Strategist Publications, Inc., 1997).

*Catch the Age Wave: A Handbook for Effective Ministry With Senior Adults*, by Win Arn and Charles Arn (Beacon Hill Press, 1999).

*Counseling Troubled Older Adults: A Handbook for Pastors and Religious Caregivers*, by Harold G. Koenig and Andrew J. Weaver (Abingdon Press, 1997).

*Engaging in Ministry With Older Adults*, by Dosia Carlson (The Alban Institute, 1997)

*Fact Book on Aging*, by Elizabeth Vierck (ABC-CLIO, Inc., 1990). This book is out of print; your local or church library may have a copy.

*Family Caregiving: Agenda for the Future*, edited by Marjorie H. Cantor (American Society on Aging, 1994).

*Global Aging Into the 21st Century* (U.S. Census Bureau, 1996).

*Guidelines for Leading Your Congregation, 1997–2000: Guiding Adult Ministries*, by Roy H. Ryan and Richard H. Gentzler, Jr. (Abingdon Press, 1996).

*How to Care for Aging Parents: A Complete Guide*, by Virginia Morris (Workman Publishing Company, Inc., 1996).

*Leading Adult Learners: Handbook for All Christian Groups*, by Delia Halverson (Abingdon Press, 1995).

*Spiritual Maturity in the Later Years*, edited by James J. Seeber (The Haworth Press, Inc., 1991).

*Visible and Vital: A Handbook for the Aging Congregation*, by Harriet Kerr Swenson (Paulist Press, 1994).

## VIDEOS FOR LEADERS OF OLDER-ADULT MINISTRY

*The Age Wave . . . Wake Up Call.* 13 minutes. Excellent video for encouraging local congregations to become involved in older-adult ministries. Available from Church Growth, Inc., P.O. Box 541, Monrovia, CA 91017 (call 626-305-1280; fax 626-305-1286); $11.95 + $3.20 shipping.

*Even to Your Old Age.* 46 minutes. Produced by the National Interfaith Coalition on Aging, this excellent video provides a positive view of "graying" congregations. Available from National Council on the Aging, 409 Third Street SW, Suite 200, Washington, DC 20024 (call 202-479-1200; fax 202-479-0735), Order #V-009; $23.00.

*Even These May Forget.* Includes 16-page guide, descriptive brochure, and 18-minute video. A video that helps congregations think about and discuss issues related to Alzheimer's Disease. Available from Alzheimer's Disease Education and Referral Center, P.O. Box 8250, Silver Spring, MD 20907-8250 (call 800-438-4380), Catalog No. A-14; $18.00.

*Live Long and Love It.* 30 minutes. Helpful resource for congregations starting older-adult ministries. Available from Church Growth, Inc., P.O. Box 541, Monrovia, CA 91017 (call 626-305-1280; fax 626-305-1286); $29.95 + $3.20 shipping.

*Aging Me . . . Aging You, Part 1: The Journey of a Lifetime.* 32 minutes. A valuable video resource for congregations beginning older-adult ministries. This is the first of two videos. Available

*ᐥᐥᐥ*

from Presbyterian Distribution Services, 100 Witherspoon
Street, Louisville, KY 40202 (call 800-524-2612), Order
#70250-94-704; $19.95.

*Aging Me . . . Aging You, Part 2: Exploring the Issues.* 30 minutes. This is the second part of the video listed above. Available
from Presbyterian Distribution Services, 100 Witherspoon
Street, Louisville, KY 40202 (call 800-524-2612), Order
#70250-95-705; $19.95.

*Aging Parents: The Family Survival Guide.* Includes 2 videos,
180-page Action Guide workbook, and QuickFind card. A
must resource for adult children who are caring for aging parents. Endorsed by the National Council on the Aging and the
American Society on Aging. Available from Lifetapes Commu-
nications (call toll-free 888-777-5585; order online at
**http://www.agingparents.com**), Order code L003-0000B for
reduced price of $84.00 plus $10.00 shipping and handling.
Also available: *Aging Parents: The Seminar*, designed for
churches who want to be in ministry with adult children who
are caring for aging parents. Licensed for public presentation.
$495.00. *Aging Parents: Planning for the Future*, 1-hour PBS
program on video; $24.95.

*Gaining a Heart of Wisdom.* 36 minutes. A beautiful video for
the spiritual growth of older adults. Available from Willow-
green Productions, P.O. Box 8738, Fort Wayne, IN 46898-8738
(call 219-490-2222); $39.95 for churches + $4.00 shipping and
handling.

*Putting Caring Into Action.* 12 minutes. A resource to help
congregations start an Interfaith Volunteer Caregivers program.
Out of print but may be available through your conference
library or your local Interfaith Volunteer Caregivers (IVC) program. For the nearest IVC program, call 1-800-350-7438.

*Program Assistant in Adult Day Care.* Includes 163-page manual and 50-minute video. This video provides information for
local congregations wanting to start an adult daycare program.

Available from National Adult Day Services Association, a unit of the National Council on the Aging, 409 Third Street SW, Suite 200, Washington, DC 20024 (call 202-479-6682; fax 202-479-0735), $82.00 + shipping and handling. Video only: $35.00 + shipping and handling. Members receive twenty percent discount.

*A Good Place to Grow Old.* Includes manual and 32-minute video. A useful video providing discussion material for older-adult ministry. Available from American Society on Aging, 833 Market Street, Suite 511, San Francisco, CA 94103-1824 (call 415-974-9600; order by Internet at **http://www.asaging.org**). Order #V003; $39.95 + $3.50 shipping and handling.

*The Grand Way.* Includes leader's guide and four 15- to 20-minute videos. Another useful video providing discussion material for older-adult ministry. Available from Church Growth, Inc., P.O. Box 541, Monrovia, CA 91017 (call 626-305-1280; fax 626-305-1286); $124.50 + $6.50 shipping.

## BOOKS FOR OLDER ADULTS

*Autumn Wisdom: A Book of Readings*, by Richard L. Morgan (Upper Room Books, 1995). Contains eighty-one meditations and stories about a diverse group of older adults, offering inspirational reflections and insightful realities associated with aging.

*A Deepening Love Affair: The Gift of God in Later Life*, by Jane Marie Thibault (Upper Room Books, 1993). Provides a rich perspective on spirituality in life's later years by showing ways to become aware of our gifts, the barriers that keep us from discovering our gifts, and our responses to these gifts.

*From Grim to Green Pastures: Meditations for the Sick and Their Caregivers*, by Richard L. Morgan (Upper Room, 1994). Insightful meditations for the sick and their caregivers.

*I Never Found That Rocking Chair: God's Call at Retirement*, by Richard L. Morgan (Upper Room Books, 1993). Thoughtful and enriching meditations revealing retirement as a time for rewarding involvement and deepening spirituality.

*No Wrinkles on the Soul: A Book of Readings for Older Adults*, by Richard L. Morgan (Upper Room Books, 1990). A collection of sixty inspiring devotions for the many lifestyles of older adults.

*Remembering Your Story: A Guide to Spiritual Autobiography*, by Richard L. Morgan (Upper Room Books, 1996). Designed primarily for small groups, this book helps older adults engage in a spiritual autobiography through life review.

*Winter Grace: Spirituality and Aging*, by Kathleen Fischer (Upper Room Books, 1998). An excellent resource showing how the losses that accompany aging can lead to freedom and new life.

*With Faces to the Evening Sun: Faith Stories From the Nursing Home*, by Richard L. Morgan (Upper Room Books, 1998). This book of meditations is written for nursing home residents and their families.

# UNITED METHODIST COMMITTEE ON OLDER ADULT MINISTRIES

An additional resource to assist local congregations, districts, and conferences in ministry with older adults is the United Methodist Committee on Older Adult Ministries. Approximately twenty-five people from across The United Methodist Church serve on this committee in an effort to advocate, network, plan, and resource older-adult ministries. Legislation establishing the Committee on Older Adult Ministries was first approved by General Conference action in 1992. The most recent legislation concerning the committee was in 1996. If you would like to know more about the United Methodist Committee on Older Adult Ministries, you are invited to contact the General Board of Discipleship at Office of Adult Ministries, General Board of Discipleship, P.O. Box 340003, Nashville, TN 37203-0003. The following paragraphs,

*✻✻✻*

taken from *The Book of Discipline—1996*, describe the purpose, responsibilities, and membership of the Committee:

1. There shall be a **Committee on Older Adult Ministries,** which shall be administratively related to the General Board of Discipleship.

2. *Purpose*—The committee will provide a forum for information sharing, cooperative planning, and joint program endeavors as determined in accordance with the responsibilities and objectives of the participating agencies. The committee shall serve as an advocate for older adult concerns and issues and shall serve to support ministries by, with, and for older adults throughout The United Methodist Church and in the larger society.

3. *Responsibilities*—The responsibilities of the committee shall include the following:

*a*) Identify the needs, concerns, and potential contributions of older adults.

*b*) Promote a plan of comprehensive ministry by, with, and for older adults in local churches that includes spiritual growth, education, training, mission, service, and fellowship.

*c*) Support the development of resources that will undergird local church ministries by, with, and for older adults.

*d*) Advocate development and implementation of policies and service designed to impact systems and concepts that adversely affect older adults.

*e*) Educate and keep before the Church the lifelong process of aging, with emphasis on the quality of life, intergenerational understanding, and faith development.

*f*) Encourage the development of resources and programs that can be used by annual conferences, jurisdictions, and the denomination at large in training and equipping older adults for new roles in the ministry and mission of the Church.

*g*) Serve as focal point for supplying information and guidelines on Older Adult Ministries to local churches.

*h*) Encourage coordination among agencies responsible for the development of resources, programs, and policies relating to older adult ministries.

4. *Membership*—The committee shall be composed of one board member and one staff member from each of the following agencies: the General Board of Discipleship, the General Board of Global Min-

istries, the General Board of Church and Society, the General Board of Higher Education and Ministry, and the General Council on Ministries; one member (board or staff) from the Commission on the Status and Role of Women, one from the Commission on Religion and Race, and one from the Commission on United Methodist Men; one retired bishop representing the Council of Bishops; one central conference representative; five older adults, one to be selected by each jurisdictional College of Bishops; and no more than five additional members to be selected by the committee for expertise, professional qualifications, and/or inclusiveness (racial and ethnic, disability, age, gender, laity, clergy, or geographic distribution). Staff members will provide appropriate liaison and reports to their respective agencies. They will have voice but not vote.

5. *Meetings*—The committee will meet at least once a year in conjunction with a meeting of the General Board of Discipleship.

(From *The Book of Discipline of The United Methodist Church—1996*. Copyright © 1996 by The United Methodist Publishing House, ¶1119. Used by permission.)

# CHAPTER SIX
# SAMPLE FORMS AND OTHER HELPS

## FACTS ABOUT AGING: A QUIZ

**True or False**

_____ 1. Most older people are pretty much alike.

_____ 2. Different parts of the body age at different rates.

_____ 3. The life expectancy for women is, on the average, six to seven years longer than for men.

_____ 4. With older people, all five senses tend to decline.

_____ 5. In 1995, more than one-third of the people sixty-five years of age and older in the United States had incomes below the poverty level.

_____ 6. The United States ranks in the top five countries in terms of longest life expectancy.

_____ 7. People 65 years of age and older made up 12.6 percent of the 1990 United States population.

_____ 8. By the year 2030, older people will make up about fifty percent of the total United States population.

_____ 9. The majority of older adults in the United States consider their general health to be good, very good, or excellent.

_____ 10. In 1996, the United States ranked in the top ten countries for having the highest percentage of population age sixty and older.

_____ 11. Most older adults in the United States live in "family-type" settings (with spouses or with others, such as children, relatives, or friends).

_____ 12. The majority of older adults worry about death.

_____ 13. People sixty-five years of age and older who live with others visit their doctor more often than older people who live alone.

_____ 14. People naturally recognize that they are old.

_____ 15. Most older adults feel satisfied with their life.

_____ 16. Only five percent of older adults in the United States are living in nursing homes.

_____ 17. As a result of our aging society and "graying" churches, United Methodist seminaries have begun requiring course work in gerontology for all students.

_____ 18. As people grow older, their ability to learn decreases.

# FACTS ABOUT AGING: QUIZ ANSWERS

1. FALSE: Older adults are the least homogeneous group of all age groups. They have had a variety of life experiences, with differing backgrounds, work experiences, educational levels, and so forth.

2. TRUE: Age does not have a uniform effect on different organs of the body even in the same individual. For example, the heart may age faster than the lungs.

3. TRUE: Average life expectancy for a woman is approximately seventy-nine years; for a man, about seventy-two.

4. TRUE: Reduced senses are due to the general reduced capacity of the sensory system to receive and transmit messages.

5. FALSE: About 10.5 percent of the people 65 years of age and older had an income below poverty level in 1995.

6. FALSE: For women, the United States ranks twenty-first; for men, nineteenth. Some countries with a higher life expectancy are Australia, Canada, Denmark, France, Greece, Italy, Japan, Netherlands, New Zealand, Norway, and Spain.

7. TRUE: This is true according to the U.S. Bureau of the Census.

8. FALSE: Twenty-two percent is the expected figure for 2030.

9. TRUE: Over seventy percent said excellent, very good, or good. Less than thirty percent said fair or poor.

10. FALSE: The United States ranked twenty-fifth, with 16.5 percent of its population 60 years of age and older. The top ten countries were Italy, 22.3 percent; Greece, 22.3 percent;

Sweden, 21.9 percent; Belgium, 21.5 percent; Spain, 21.2 percent; Bulgaria, 21.2 percent; Japan, 20.9 percent; Germany, 20.9 percent; United Kingdom, 20.5 percent; and France, 20.3 percent.

11. <u>TRUE</u>: Sixty-eight percent of older noninstitutionalized adults live in a "family-type" setting.

12. <u>FALSE</u>: Recent studies have shown that approximately twenty-four percent of people sixty-five years of age and older worry about death, compared to fifty-five percent of the eighteen- to twenty-four-year-old age group.

13. <u>FALSE</u>: Those living with others visit the doctor an average of 4.5 times a year; those living alone visit the doctor an average of 7 times a year.

14. <u>FALSE</u>: Fifty-seven percent of Americans think they look younger than they are, and sixty-six percent say they feel young for their age.

15. <u>TRUE</u>: Seventy-two percent of people sixty-five and older feel satisfied with life.

16. <u>TRUE</u>: Only five percent of older adults are in nursing homes at any given time.

17. <u>FALSE</u>: Although there is steady growth in our aging population, United Methodist seminaries do not require course work in gerontology.

18. <u>FALSE</u>: Older adults can learn anything if given adequate time, understanding, and circumstances. While older people can learn as well as younger people, they learn in different ways.

✿

# OLDER-ADULT SURVEY FORM

Before using this survey, the local church volunteer should

1. contact the older adult being interviewed, establishing an agreed-upon day and time for the interview;
2. identify who you are upon arriving for the interview;
3. give the person being interviewed a copy of this survey form to follow as you read over each question, pausing long enough for the participant to respond to each question.

Name: _____

Date: _____

Address: _____

_____

Telephone: _____

Interviewer's Name: _____

**Mark all appropriate responses.**

1. Gender: ❑ Female   ❑ Male

2. Birth Date: _____

3. Marital Status:    ❑ Single   ❑ Married
                      ❑ Widowed   ❑ Divorced

4. Do you live alone? ❑ Yes   ❑ No
   If no, with whom do you live? _____

5. In the event of an emergency, if you needed help or became ill or disabled, is there someone you could turn to for assistance? ❑ Yes   ❑ No

   Name of contact person: _____

Address of contact person: _____

_____

Telephone number of contact person: _____

6. During this past week,
   how many times did someone come to visit you? _____
   how many times did you go to visit someone else? _____
   how many times did you go shopping? _____
   how many times did you talk with a friend or relative on
   the phone? _____

7. What problems, if any, do you experience with the place
   where you live? _____

   _____

   _____

8. How do you rate your general health?
   ❑ Excellent  ❑ Good  ❑ Fair  ❑ Poor

9. Were you employed outside the home? ❑ Yes  ❑ No
   If yes, what was your occupation? _____

10. Are you able to attend worship services at church?
    ❑ Yes  ❑ No
    How often do you attend?
    ❑ Weekly  ❑ Monthly  ❑ Occasionally
    ❑ Other _____

11. Transportation:
    a. I need transportation to: ❑ church  ❑ work
       ❑ doctor's office  ❑ shopping  ❑ other _____
    b. I could help transport others to _____

    _____

12. Home repair and minor maintenance service:
    a. I need help with: ❏ mowing grass  ❏ painting
       ❏ plumbing  ❏ moving items  ❏ carpentry
       ❏ installing locks  ❏ other _____
    b. I could help with home repairs by _____
    _____

13. Home chore service:
    a. I need help with: ❏ sewing  ❏ cooking  ❏ cleaning
       ❏ laundry  ❏ writing letters  ❏ grocery shopping
       ❏ other _____
    b. I could help with home chore service by _____
    _____

14. Healthcare service:
    a. I need information about: ❏ medical care
       ❏ dental care  ❏ home healthcare  ❏ other _____
    b. I could help with healthcare by _____
    _____

15. Legal and financial service:
    a. I need help with:  ❏ Social Security  ❏ will planning
       ❏ Medicare/Medicaid  ❏ retirement planning
       ❏ budget planning  ❏ other _____
    b. I could help with legal and financial counsel by _____
    _____

16. Personal contacts:
    a. I would like: ❏ daily telephone calls  ❏ friendly visitors
       ❏ cards and letters from church members
       ❏ other _____
    b. I could help with personal contacts by _____
    _____

17. Religious services:
    a. I would like: ❏ pastoral counseling   ❏ lay visitation
       ❏ Holy Communion   ❏ Bible study/devotional materials
       ❏ other _____
    b. I could help with religious services by _____
       _____

18. Educational services:
    a. I am interested in: ❏ large-print books   ❏ home safety
       ❏ audio books   ❏ video films   ❏ computer/Internet
       ❏ other _____
    b. I could help with educational services by _____
       _____

19. Fellowship activities:
    a. I am interested in: ❏ field trips   ❏ group games
       ❏ exercise classes   ❏ fellowship dinners
       ❏ other _____
    b. I could help with fellowship activities by _____
       _____

20. List other programs the church should provide for older
    people: _____
    _____
    _____

21. List services not already mentioned above that you could
    provide for others: _____
    _____
    _____

꧁꧂

# LOCAL CHURCH PROGRAM
# ASSESSMENT FORM

1. Church Name: _____

   Church Address: _____

   _____

2. What is the total membership of your church congregation?

   _____

3. How many people in your congregation are in the following age groups:

| | |
|---|---|
| 55–64 _____ | Percentage of total membership _____ |
| 65–74 _____ | Percentage of total membership _____ |
| 75–84 _____ | Percentage of total membership _____ |
| 85+ _____ | Percentage of total membership _____ |
| Total _____ | Total percentage _____ |

4. How many of the sixty-five-and-over age group in your church
   • need transportation help? _____
   • need extra visiting? _____
   • are homebound? _____
   • are residents of long-term care facilities? _____
   • need other kinds of special assistance? _____

5. Do you have at least one social/fellowship group especially for older adults? ❑ Yes ❑ No
   If yes, is it run by: ❑ older adults? ❑ others?
   If others, who? _____

6. Do you have a group of volunteers to drive people, if required, to: _____
   ❑ medical clinic or doctor's office?
   ❑ dental office?

❏ pharmacy?
❏ grocery store?
❏ other? _____

7. Does your church have the following:
   ❏ tape recordings of church services for homebound people?
   ❏ ramp access to sanctuary/social hall/classrooms?
   ❏ Meals-on-Wheels or other meal delivery program?
   ❏ minor maintenance and home repair service?
   ❏ home chore service?
   ❏ parish nurse program?
   ❏ exercise/aerobics classes for older adults?
   ❏ cooking and nutrition classes for older adults?
   ❏ respite care relievers program?
   ❏ telephone reassurance program?
   ❏ adult daycare center?
   ❏ prayer concern chains?
   ❏ emergency hot line?
   ❏ support groups?
   ❏ older-adult recognition service?
   ❏ accessible restrooms?

8. Approximately how many older adults are doing volunteer
   work in your church? _____
   Total hours per week _____ , month _____ , year _____

9. Do any of your church organizations arrange trips, movies,
   parties, or other forms of entertainment for older adults?
   ❏ Yes  ❏ No
   If yes, which organizations? _____

   _____

10. Does your church minister to the needs of older people in
    your community who live alone but are not church mem-
    bers or attenders? ❏ Yes  ❏ No

11. Do you have a list of volunteers who visit older parishioners? ❑ Yes ❑ No
Do they visit: ❑ hospital patients? ❑ homebound people? ❑ nursing home residents?

12. Are older adults well represented on the governing board and other committees of your church? ❑ Yes ❑ No

13. Does your church offer the following classes/seminars for adults and older adults:
❑ grief and loss?
❑ spiritual growth?
❑ death and dying?
❑ marriage communication?
❑ retirement planning?
❑ caregiving?
❑ teacher training?
❑ volunteer opportunities?
❑ pre-retirement seminars?
❑ adult children caring for aging parents?
❑ other?
Please specify:

_____

14. Do older adults participate in the following ministries:

a. teaching in local church? ❑ Yes ❑ No
If yes, with
❑ children?
❑ youth?
❑ young adults?
❑ middle adults?
❑ older adults?
❑ other? _____

b. volunteering in local elementary school? ❑ Yes ❑ No

c. volunteering in after-school programs for children?
❑ Yes   ❑ No

d. serving in worship? ❑ Yes   ❑ No
   If yes, as:
   ❑ ushers?
   ❑ greeters?
   ❑ liturgists/lay readers?
   ❑ song leader?
   ❑ choir soloists?
   ❑ other? _____

e. assisting in church office? ❑ Yes   ❑ No
   If yes, do they help with the preparation of
   ❑ weekly bulletins?
   ❑ newsletters?
   ❑ church directories?
   ❑ typing?
   ❑ mailings?
   ❑ other? _____

f. participating in mission opportunities? ❑ Yes   ❑ No
   If yes, do they participate in
   ❑ local mission projects?
   ❑ missions program?
   ❑ other? _____

g. other areas? Please specify:

_____
_____
_____
_____

✿

# LOCAL CHURCH PROGRAM
# EVENT SURVEY FORM

Identify a program involving older adults in your church.
Use a different sheet for each program.

Program Name: _____

Program Dates: From _____ to _____

Brief description of the program: _____

_____

_____

_____

What committee or organization is responsible for the program?

_____

Who provides leadership for the program? (Be specific.)

_____

_____

_____

How many volunteers provide leadership for the program?

_____

Who participates in the program? (Whom does this program serve?) _____

_____

_____

What facilities and resources are needed? _____

_____

How much was budgeted for the program? _____

How much was actually spent? _____

Do participants pay a fee? ❑ Yes ❑ No
If yes, how much per person? _____

What impact does this program make on the church and/or community? _____

_____

_____

What are the church's future plans for this program?

_____

_____

Person completing this form: _____

Date: _____

# COMMUNITY SOCIAL SERVICE
# AGENCY SURVEY FORM

Name of social service agency: _____

Contact person: _____

Position: _____

Address: _____

_____

Telephone: _____

Fax: _____

E-mail address: _____

Today's date: _____

Person completing this form: _____

Brief description of the agency: _____

_____

_____

Is the agency: ❏ non-profit?  ❏ for profit?  ❏ other?

_____

What services are available for older adults? _____

_____

_____

What are the eligibility requirements for older adults?

_____

_____

How many older adults are receiving services? _____

What costs or fees are paid by older adults? _____

Are the agency's present facilities adequate for its program?
❏ Yes  ❏ No

Are volunteers used? ❏ Yes  ❏ No

If yes, how do they serve? _____

_____

What unmet needs of older adults has the agency discovered?

_____

Does the agency have plans to meet these unmet needs?    ·
❏ Yes  ❏ No

What could the church do to assist the agency in its program?

_____

On the back of this form, please list other observations and comments. Attach any brochures or other materials distributed by this social service agency.

# JOB DESCRIPTION: LOCAL CHURCH COORDINATOR OF OLDER-ADULT MINISTRIES

**Task:**

1. The task of the local church coordinator of older-adult ministries shall be to assist the local church congregation in its ministry with older adults.

2. The coordinator shall be responsible for coordinating the primary task of the local congregation with older adults.

3. The coordinator is charged with the task of planning and coordinating an intentional ministry by, with, and for older adults in the local church.

4. The coordinator does not run the older-adult ministries. Rather, he or she facilitates and coordinates the work of others.

**Qualities:**

The following qualities may enhance one's ability to be an effective local church coordinator of older-adult ministries:

- **articulate**—a person who can communicate well with others;
- **faithful**—a person who is involved in the life of a local church congregation and is growing in his or her Christian faith;
- **knowledgeable**—a person who is knowledgeable about older-adult concerns and aging issues and is knowledgeable about the organization of The United Methodist Church;
- **resourceful**—a person who is capable of enlisting others to participate in events and programs and is capable of acquiring resources and information available to the faith community.

**Responsibilities:**

The following list of responsibilities is a guideline for carrying out the work of the local church coordinator of older-adult ministries.

1. Work closely with your church's
   - pastor
   - church lay leader

- chairperson of the church council (administrative board/council on ministries or administrative council)
- chairpeople of the nurture and outreach committees
- chairperson of the Christian education committee
- coordinators of adult and family ministries

2. Help older adults relate to God by inviting them to become disciples of Jesus Christ, and to equip them and send them out in service in the world.

3. Study the needs and concerns of older adults in the local church congregation and community.

4. Serve as chairperson of the older-adult council.

5. Conduct regular meetings of the older-adult council and appoint committees and task forces as necessary to carry out the work of older-adult ministries.

6. Organize an older-adult survey file for all older adults in the congregation and develop a process for using the information.

7. Survey the needs of older adults, church programs, and church facilities as each relates to older-adult ministries.

8. Coordinate with the church council the planning and implementation of a unified and comprehensive plan for ministry by, with, and for older adults.

9. Keep the needs and concerns of older adults before the church council and the local congregation.

10. Advocate on behalf of the needs and concerns of older adults in the local congregation and community.

11. Inform older adults about district and conference events and other opportunities for learning and serving in the church and community.

12. Serve as liaison with organizations, people, and resources in and beyond the local church as each relates to older adults.

13. Review and evaluate programs as they affect ministry by, with, and for older adults.

14. Continue learning and growing in the Christian faith.

15. Participate in opportunities for continued education in areas relating to older-adult ministries.

**Committees:**
The local church coordinator of older-adult ministries may serve on the following committees:
- church council (administrative board/council on ministries or administrative council);
- older-adult council;
- nurture and outreach committees;
- Christian education committee;
- other committees deemed necessary to carry out an intentional older-adult ministry.

# LOCAL CHURCH ACCESSIBILITY SURVEY FORM

Is your church accessible and open to all people? This brief survey form will help you identify your strengths and weaknesses. Take a few minutes and walk through your church building. What do you see? Please check all those that apply to your local church facilities:

**Church entrance and halls:**
❑ Is there a ramp or level entrance to the church door?
❑ Are there directional signs so people know where to go upon entering the church building?
❑ Is there a church directory to assist visitors in locating meeting rooms and other locations?
❑ Are there handrails at the church entrance and in halls?
❑ Are water fountains, coin telephones, bulletin boards, and so forth at a height accessible to people in wheelchairs?
❑ Are braille signs and textured doorknobs provided?
❑ Are water fountains, coin telephones, bulletin boards, and other items recessed into the wall so as not to create obstacles?

**Parking:**
❑ Are there several parking spaces marked as handicapped parking?
❑ Is the parking lot well lighted at night?
❑ Is there a level approach to the church building from the parking area or the street?
❑ Do you provide valet parking service?
❑ Are snow and ice adequately removed from walkways?
❑ Do you provide security patrol in the parking lot at night?

**Restrooms:**
❑ Do restrooms (especially toilet areas) have handrails?
❑ Are restrooms (including toilet stalls, sinks, mirrors, soap, and towels) wheelchair accessible?
❑ Are restrooms accessible to the church sanctuary, classrooms, and meeting rooms?

## Sanctuary:

- ❏ Can the sanctuary accommodate wheelchairs?
- ❏ Is there adequate lighting on the speaker's face to facilitate speech/lip reading?
- ❏ Is there adequate lighting for reading in all pews?
- ❏ Are large-print Bibles available?
- ❏ Are large-print hymnals or songbooks available?
- ❏ Are large-print worship materials (such as bulletins) available?
- ❏ Is the sound system of good quality and without dead spots?
- ❏ Are individual hearing devices for people with hearing impairments available?
- ❏ Is sign language provided during worship services?
- ❏ Are pews cushioned for added comfort?
- ❏ Are guide dogs permitted in the church sanctuary?
- ❏ Is there a temperature-controlled heating and cooling system?
- ❏ Is the altar and chancel area open and without steps for people receiving the sacrament of Holy Communion?
- ❏ Is the altar and chancel area open and without steps for people receiving the sacrament of baptism?
- ❏ Is the altar and chancel area accessible for older-adult leaders during the worship service?
- ❏ Are several places for wheelchairs provided so that wheelchair users have a choice of seating?

## Doors:

- ❏ Are exterior and interior doors easy to open?
- ❏ Do church doors swing without conflict to wheelchairs?
- ❏ Are there vertical door handles or horizontal door bars rather than slippery round knobs?

## Elevators:

- ❏ Is there an elevator or chair lift in the building?
- ❏ Do elevators have buttons low enough for wheelchair users to reach?
- ❏ Are braille signs utilized and placed between four feet six inches and five feet six inches from the floor?

**Transportation:**

❑ Does the church provide transportation for worship and church-related activities?

❑ Does the church have a van capable of transporting people in wheelchairs?

❑ Does the church have arrangements with any agency to help transport people with disabilities?

**Church administration, leadership, worship, and church school:**
Do people with disabilities participate in worship and church school as:

❑ greeters and ushers?

❑ liturgists or lay readers?

❑ choir members/soloists?

❑ lay speakers?

❑ church school teachers?

❑ class officers/leaders?

Do people with disabilities participate in and provide leadership for any of the following?

❑ church council (administrative board/council on ministries or administrative council)

❑ committees and boards

Which of the following does your church take seriously?

❑ time of day for programs planned

❑ effective communication techniques

❑ style of program presentation

❑ content of material

❑ accessibility of programs or events

❑ worship services and other special programs taped and provided to members who are unable to come to church

# HOW TO DISCOURAGE OLDER ADULTS FROM BEING PART OF YOUR CONGREGATION!

Most local churches want to welcome people into their congregations. However, without realizing it they may be pulling up the welcome mat and shutting the door to older adults. Below are ways congregations might discourage older-adult participation:

- Have poor acoustics and speak softly.
- Have pews with no cushions.
- Use only small-print hymnals and songbooks.
- Have uneven carpet and pavement.
- Don't encourage older adults to serve as liturgists or lay readers.
- Print bulletins and newsletters in small, fine print.
- Discourage older adults from serving on committees, teams, and boards.
- Use only small-print Bibles and Sunday school materials.
- Don't announce older-adult events.
- Install high, dim lighting.
- Don't use a public address system.
- Play music too loudly.
- Announce activities as "family-oriented."
- Have an altar rail that can be reached only by climbing many steps.
- Don't install hearing aid devices.
- Avoid using old, familiar, favorite hymns.
- Have only younger adults organizing older-adult ministries.
- Seat older people by themselves.
- Classify people as old or too old.
- Have a ministry aimed only at children, youth, or young families.
- Don't clear walks of ice and snow.
- Avoid installing wide doors, wheelchair lifts, accessible restrooms, handrails, and handicap parking spaces.
- Don't sweep rice from walks after weddings.

# CHECKLIST FOR SELECTING A NURSING HOME

**Observe Residents**
❑ Are residents clean, neat, and well groomed?
❑ Are residents up and out of bed?
❑ Are residents dressed in their own clothes?
❑ Are residents active and friendly?
❑ Are residents treated with dignity and respect?
❑ Do residents look and act happy?

**Observe Building**
Are the following rooms clean and in good repair?
   ❑ Residents' rooms
   ❑ Bathrooms
   ❑ Kitchen
   ❑ Lounge and visitors' area
   ❑ Activity room
❑ Are personal items such as furniture, photographs, radios, televisions, and so forth permitted in the rooms?
❑ How many people live in one room? (Does this make a difference to you?)

**Observe Staff**
❑ Is there a Registered Nurse or Licensed Practical Nurse on duty?
❑ What is the ratio of staff to residents?
❑ Do staff members smile, act friendly, and appear happy?
❑ Are staff members neat and clean?
❑ Are staff members visible and available?
Do staff members seem kind and considerate toward
   ❑ Nursing home residents?
   ❑ Visitors?
   ❑ Family members?
   ❑ Other staff members?

## Listen
❑ Do staff members speak courteously with residents?
❑ Do staff members speak to residents as adults?
❑ Do residents complain about the nursing home?
❑ Do staff complain about working conditions?

## Food
❑ Do residents have a choice in the food served?
❑ Is the dining room convenient, cheerful, and comfortable?
❑ Is the food appetizing, adequate, and attractively served?
❑ Are fresh fruits and vegetables served?
❑ Do staff or volunteers help residents who need help eating?
❑ Are snacks served throughout the day and in the evening?
❑ Are meals available for guests?

## Smell
❑ Is there a strong body odor or urine odor in the building?
❑ Is there a strong deodorant smell?

## Ask
❑ Are religious services provided?
❑ Is there a residents' council?
❑ Is there an activities program?
❑ Are physical, occupational, and/or speech therapy provided?
❑ What professionals are on the staff? (doctor, dentist, optometrist, podiatrist, chaplain, social worker)
❑ Does this facility meet personal interest needs?

## Money
❑ Is a deposit required?
❑ Are provisions available to handle personal funds?
❑ What other costs are involved? (Medication, beauty salon/barber, activity fees, laundry, snacks)
❑ Can residents stay when their own funds have run out?
❑ How often does the resident, family member, or guardian receive an itemized accounting of personal funds?
❑ In the event of death, what happens to any unused funds?

# A LITANY ON AGING

Leader: Then the LORD said, "My spirit shall not abide in mortals forever, for they are flesh; their days shall be one hundred twenty years." (Genesis 6:3)

*People: Dear Lord, we do need time to grow.*

Leader: Honor your father and your mother, so that your days may be long in the land that the LORD your God is giving you. (Exodus 20:12)

*People: We pray that the long years will be good years.*

Leader: The glory of youths is their strength, but the beauty of the aged is their gray hair. (Proverbs 20:29)

*People: Give us strength and experience.*

Leader: Remember the days of old, consider the years long past; ask your father, and he will inform you; your elders, and they will tell you. (Deuteronomy 32:7)

*People: Remind us to ask, and teach us to listen.*

Leader: Gray hair is a crown of glory; it is gained in a righteous life. (Proverbs 16:31)

*People: Day by day we strive to be more holy.*

Leader: Listen to your father who begot you, and do not despise your mother when she is old. (Proverbs 23:22)

*People: We are grateful for parents who teach and nurture in love.*

Leader: So even to old age and gray hairs, O God, do not forsake me, until I proclaim your might to all the generations to come. (Psalm 71:18)

*People: We love to tell the story of Jesus and his love.*

Leader: In old age they still produce fruit; they are always green and full of sap. (Psalm 92:14)

*People: We must look past the wrinkles and see the soul.*

Leader: You who are younger must accept the authority of the elders. (1 Peter 5:5)

*People: Yes, we too will soon know and understand. Give us wisdom so that we may serve others as we have been served. Amen.*

# A STATEMENT OF FAITH ON AGING

Leader: Aging is a lifelong process from birth to death that encompasses the whole span of life and not merely that of its final stages.

Group: *We affirm that God is our Creator, the giver of life, who calls us into a divine-human fellowship, and who continually challenges us to new possibilities.*

Leader: We believe that we are under the providential care of God from birth to death.

Group: *We affirm our faith in Jesus Christ, who makes all things new and who offers life and hope to people of all ages on their continuing pilgrimage of faith.*

Leader: The grace we experience through faith in Christ is the source of self-transcendence in all stages of our life.

Group: *We affirm our belief in the Holy Spirit as God's presence with us for comfort, guidance, and strength.*

Leader: Confident of the Divine Presence in our life, we are called to face the gains and losses of advancing years as opportunities for spiritual understanding and growth.

Group: *Conscious of God's redemptive love in our life, we dare to stand with others, not only in their strength but in their weakness, failure, and sin.*

Leader: We believe that we are called to be present with others, including older people with special interests and needs, and to reach out in love and in caring relationships to them.

Group: *We would capture a vision of God's promised reign with peace, justice, and grace for our life and for our world. Older adults should have the opportunity to give fully of themselves in making our communities and world more loving and just.*

Leader: We believe that the church as the body of Christ is called to reconcile people of all ages to one another and to God. Older adults, no less than others, are called to be agents of reconciliation.

Group: *Older adults have gifts, graces, experience, and skills to share in the transmission of our faith heritage and in their response to the mission to which God calls them and the church.*

Leader: Like others, older adults are not simply to *be* served but to *serve.*

Group: *The church is called to an intentional ministry by, with, and for older adults.*

Leader: The church is called to respond to the needs of older people, to call forth their creative powers, to address their longing for wholeness in all of life's relationships, and to support them in the critical hours of loneliness, illness, and death.

Group: *We believe that older adults must have the opportunity to reaffirm their faith and commitment to Christ and the church at this significant period in their life, to be nurtured in the faith, and to rejoice in the Christian hope. We also believe that it is imperative that older adults have a voice in planning ministries and forming policies related to their own age group. We join them and one another in joy and in sorrow, in life and in death, and face the future with the assurance that God is with us. Thanks be to God!*

(Based on "The Theological Response," *Statement on Aging,* General Board of Global Ministries, The United Methodist Church.)

# A WORKSHOP MODEL
# FOR USING THIS RESOURCE

Follow the outline below for planning and conducting a two-hour workshop using the book *Designing an Older-Adult Ministry*.

| Time | Topic | Activities |
|------|-------|-----------|
| 15 min. | Welcome/ Devotions | A. Devotions<br>B. Use "A Litany on Aging" (pages 90–91). |
| 10 min. | Getting Acquainted Time | A. If there are any participants who don't know one another, have participants introduce themselves to the group. |
| 45 min. | **PART 1:** Facts and Feelings About Aging | A. Before ministry can be planned, developed, and implemented, attitudes and needs of aging people must be considered. You may want to have class members do any one or two of the following:<br>• "Facts About Aging: A Quiz" (pages 65–66);<br>• "Self-Awareness Inventory" (page 22);<br>• "Personal Reflection" (page 23);<br>• Review student responses together. |

| | | |
|---|---|---|
| | | B. Discuss losses and gains associated with growing older (pages 25–27). Have participants identify additional losses and gains. List responses on newsprint.<br>C. Review faith needs of older adults (pages 29–30). List responses on newsprint. |
| 20 min. | **PART 2:**<br>Forming a<br>Working<br>Council | A. Identify the work of an older-adult council (pages 40–41).<br>B. Identify barriers to older-adult ministry. Use "How to Discourage Older Adults From Being Part of Your Congregation!" (page 87).<br>C. Discuss the idea of a mission statement (pages 35, 40). |
| 25 min. | **PART 3:**<br>Discovering<br>Needs and<br>Interests of<br>Older Adults | A. Discuss the importance of an older-adult survey (pages 32–34).<br>B. Share with the class the model "Older-Adult Survey Form" (pages 69–72).<br>C. In small groups, develop a local church program assessment questionnaire (pages 34–35, 73–76). |
| 30 min. | **PART 4:**<br>Developing<br>Programs for<br>Older Adults | A. Describe ministry models: S.E.N.I.O.R.S. Program (pages 46–48) and Shepherd's Center (pages 48–49). |

| | | |
|---|---|---|
| | | B. Discuss selected ministry program models (pages 49–52).<br>C. List on chalkboard or newsprint additional ideas of participants. |
| 5 min. | Closing | A. Use "A Statement of Faith on Aging" (pages 92–93).<br>B. Prayer and sending forth |